RAVES FOR
PRESS BONERS

More Press Boners is an original Pocket Book edition.

Also by Earle Tempel

PRESS BONERS

Published by Pocket Books

 Are there paperbound books you want but cannot find in your retail stores?

MORE
PRESS
BONERS

Compiled by
EARLE TEMPEL

☆☆☆☆☆☆☆☆☆

Another mirth-provoking selection of humorous typographical errors as made in the columns of thousands of newspapers and other news media throughout the civilized (?) world

PUBLISHED BY POCKET  BOOKS NEW YORK

MORE PRESS BONERS

A Pocket Book edition
1st printing .... July, 1968

This book is respectfully dedicated to you, the purchaser. It shows three things: you know a good book when you see it, you appreciate humor, and, perhaps the most important of all, you *had* fifty cents!

FOREWORD

MORE PRESS BONERS is the second of the PRESS BONERS books. For those of you who were lucky enough to get a copy of the first book at your newsstands during the past few months, you will know that this book is a comprehensive collection of humorous mistakes made by the publishing media during the past fifty years. I'm sure you will agree with me that the book is very funny.

Due to the many excellent book reviews given to PRESS BONERS by the leading newspapers in the United States and Canada, plus nationwide radio and TV "plugs" by topflight radio and TV stars, Durward Kirby and Art Linkletter among them, it has often been impossible to obtain PRESS BONERS at your local newsstand. We'll hope MORE PRESS BONERS will also tickle YOUR funnybone!

EARLE TEMPEL

Miss O'Hayer has been raising birds for many years and is credited with having the largest parateets in the state.

New York (N.Y.) *Times*

Eggs as big as hailstones dropped for about ten minutes during the storm.

Fort Smith (Ark.) *News*

The district has no figures as to the number of married students who are pregnant. Almost all of them are girls.

Redondo Beach (Calif.) *Daily Breeze*

The Aga Khan, interviewed on the subject of what religion Rita Hayworth's child will be reared in, "rapped his can on the floor for emphasis and said: 'Moslem—then it won't need a Papal dispensation.' "

Pittsburgh (Pa.) *Sun-Telegraph*

Their meetings were frank, informal, hard-bargaining sessions. The negotiators worked in shirtsleeves, ties loosened, sitting in chairs and on the floor, drinking plenty of coffee. Some even took off their shoes. P U

New York (N.Y.) *Times*

Prospective parents are advised that in the future birth certificates must be recorded in the city or town clerk's office where the birth occurs.

Wellman (Calif.) *Journal*

John Dyer reports that he has been successful in raising a family of eight children, equally divided into four girls and four boys. We believe this is a very good record for a man with only one arm.

Pierre (S.D.) *Capital Journal*

The daughter of the local candy store keeper, as the virgin in this year's production of the Passion Play at Oberammergau, has already started her rehearsal. She is the first blonde virgin for a century.

New York (N.Y.) *Journal-American*

The Florida legislature has approved a bill making possession of more than one gallon of moonshine whiskey a felony and possession of less than one gallon a misdemeanor.

(New York, N.Y.) United Press International

Because of the shape of the building and the absence of the metallic substance, the acoustic properties of the Tabernacle are marvelous. A pint dropped at the front of the auditorium can be heard distinctly at the extreme rear of the building.

Salt Lake City (Utah) *Telegram*

In New York State alone, the federal emergency relief has bought twelve cabbages to fill twelve train-loads of one hundred cars each.

Pittsburgh (Pa.) *Post-Gazette*

A St. Louis firm has invented an automatic control which lowers the TV sound when you pick up the phone, raises it to abnormal again when you replace the receiver.

Youngstown (Ohio) *Vindicator*

The rule in most cases is that the vehicle on the right has the right-of-way, regardless of whether it is on the right or left.

Albany (N.Y.) *Times-Union*

The local Lions Club has 74 members. It was organized last November and since that time has become one of the strangest civic clubs in the area.

Wildwood (N.J.) *Leader*

A bookie was escorted by two detectives after a raid when a customer approached the trio on the sidewalk and tried to get a bed down.

Los Angeles (Calif.) *Herald-Examiner*

Michigan motorists are warned to leave accident victims at the scene until police arrive. Until then, though, it would be considerate to visit them daily.

Canton (Ohio) *Repository*

"One of the major successes of the Peace Corps is dispelling the image of the 'Ugly American,' " she declared. "Underpopulation is a big problem in Bolivia and the Peace Corps supplies the necessary manpower while eliminating the middle man."

Rochester (N.Y.) *Democrat & Chronicle*

Today, on the 166th anniversary of the birth of Samuel Finley Breese Morse—who sent that first code telegram—the number of Morse operators in Greater Cleveland could be counted on the fingers of one man's hand. There are only nine.

Cleveland (Ohio) *Plain Dealer*

Mrs. and Mrs. David Oldt and Mr. and Mrs. Luther Reichley spent Sunday at Philadelphia to see Miss Irene Oldt and other sights at that place.

Miffinburg (Pa.) *Telegraph*

The ladies of the Cherry Street Church have discarded clothing of all kinds. Call at 44 North Cherry Street for inspection.

Philadelphia (Pa.) *Church Bulletin*

William Andrews returned home yesterday from the hospital, where his left leg was placed in a cast following a fracture of the right ankle.

Malone (N.Y.) *Telegram*

An errant youth is on his way to a new tart tonight, thanks to sympathetic citizens here.

Charleston (S.C.) *News and Courier*

The newest thing in railroad equipment is the shower-bath for women in the observation car.

Chicago (Ill.) *Tribune*

Mrs. Samuel Calcotte entertained at luncheon Monday, honoring Mrs. Dale McIntyre, who was again celebrating her 29th birthday.

Drayton Plains (Mich.) *Lakeland Tribune*

The Book-Lovers Club had a get-together with the husbands of members Thursday evening. Following dinner the group went to the home of a member to watch television.

Mankato (Minn.) *Free Press*

The Dads of Foreign Wars met last week at the home of Mr. and Mrs. Frank Adams for a card party. Mrs. Thomas McCombie was the door prize.

Macomb County (Mich.) *South Macomb News*

Our paper carried the notice last week that Mr. John Doe is a defective in the police force. This was a typographical error. Mr. Doe is really a detective in the police farce.

Annapolis (Md.) *Log*

Herbert Holeman, twenty-eight, of 417 New York Avenue northwest, who was injured today when the automobile truck on which he was riding collided with a street car on Connecticut Avenue near Porter Street northwest, died yesterday at Emergency Hospital from internal injuries.

Washington (D.C.) *Post*

The annual report of the town auditors, Knust, Everett and Cambria, has been completed and is not available for inspection at the Town Clerk's office.

Middletown (Conn.) *Press*

WARNING: Do not deposit coin in making a local call until the party on the other end answers. This is signified by an end of the ringing and a blank sound.

Fort Smith (Ark.) *Times Record*

Four wheels are so firmly established in Europe that a cat not so equipped is a noticeable exception.

Amarillo (Tex.) *News*

Charles Scates had the misfortune to get a foot badly washed a few days ago.

Lynchburg (Va.) *Advance*

Wakefield is a 170-pound 6 footer who was given a $35,000 bonus by the Cardinals in 1961. His minor league record is undistinguished, but Met scouts reported favorably on his potential and the Cards thought enough of him to protect him from the forthcoming draft by putting him on their rooster.

New York (N.Y.) *Times*

She was one of hundreds of flapjack eaters at the club's annual pancake festival. Each contributed $1 for all they could eat. By noon, the cakes had been eaten by 1,600 persons, including a 17 year old high school boy who tucked away 22 pancakes and an 89 year old resident.

Chicago (Ill.) *Tribune*

Mr. and Mrs. John North Willys announced the engagement of their debatable daughter, Miss Virgin A Willys, to Mr. Luis Marcelino de Aguire of Buenos Aires.

New York (N.Y.) *Herald Tribune*

In a county which has a population of approximately 40,000 there are only twenty-three paid officers, of whom eighteen are assigned to day duty, leaving only five on the night shirt.

Washington (D.C.) *Post*

Frank Williams, an unemployed printer, died Tuesday. Mr. Williams was arrested yesterday after an autopsy showed traces of arsenic poisoning in his body.

New York (N.Y.) *World-Telegram & Sun*

Indians sent wireless signals by placing a hollow hog in a river and beating the uppermost end with a stick; the vibrations carried many miles in the water.

Pittsburgh (Pa.) *Press*

He is the son of Admiral Thomas C. Hart, who is now somewhere in the Pacific in command of the Asiatic fleet and Mrs. Hart.

Washington (D.C.) *Post*

The Central Ohio Hiking Club of the YMCA will sponsor an excursion to Pelee Island in Lake Erie on Saturday and Sunday. The group will travel to Sandusky by bus, go by plane to Pelee, and return to Sandusky by boat.

Columbus (Ohio) *State Journal*

Mr. Hammond Kinnick, safety engineer for the highway department, was injured in an auto accident while on the way to Greensville High School to deliver a lecture entitled "Safe-Driving—It Pays."

Springfield (Mo.) *Leader & Press*

Born to Mr. and Mrs. Herbert P. Wilson, a fine boy Wednesday morning. After the baby was born he went downtown and the boys celebrated the occasion by burning his hat.

Kansas City (Mo.) *Star*

The hearing was to find whether the deceased was sane enough to stand trial.

Vancouver (Canada) *Sun*

Reporting to police the loss of $20, she said the money was concealed in her stocking, and the loss was discovered soon after the departure of a vacuum-cleaner salesman who had been demonstrating his line.

Grand Rapids (Mich.) *Herald*

He underwent a third transfusion last night, to offset a singing spell.

Philadelphia (Pa.) *Inquirer*

Mrs. Phillips, wife and adopted daughter of the pastor, was present.

Louisville (Ky.) *Times*

The Telephone Company announced that in accordance with our new convenient All Number Dialing System, your new number is 5839218352274061, Area

Code 8153900627, and that due to increased business prosperity making possible more investments for more profit, we are able to announce a rate increase.

St. Louis (Mo.) *Post-Dispatch*

Ex-Governor James, who is an attorney for the complainants, is working without thought or remuneration.

Laceyville (Pa.) *Wyoming County Courier*

The Internal Revenue has called in several local businessmen to straighten out their income lax.

Little Rock (Ark.) *Gazette*

The body lay in state at the family home here today while thousands of friends and relatives passed the beer.

Louisville (Ky.) *Courier-Journal*

Why, it would kill the average man to look after one three-year-old boy for a week at a stretch, something a woman does every day.

Evansville (Ind.) *Press*

Miss Statia Watkins will entertain the members of the pan-hellenic association with a bridge party at her home on Woodford avenue on Saturday afternoon. She will be arrested by Mrs. John Hillard and Miss Frances Hinson.

Fort Myers (Fla.) *News Press*

She started with an ugly old bed, with wooden head and footboards. Her husband cut the footboard off, and from then on she was on her own. She padded

17

the headboard with an old quilted bedpan, then drew around it to make the pattern for the slip cover.

Washington (D.C.) *Times-Herald*

To keep drawers from swelling and hard to pull out, use paste wax on your bottoms once a year.

Van Buren (Ark.) *Press Argus*

Weather Report: In 24 hour period ended at 5:30 a.m. today, the maximum was 83, the minimum 56.
Forecast: Considerable

Sacramento (Calif.) *Bee*

Due to the many unexplained happenings in this part of the country the past week, many hunters feel that it is unsafe for them to sleep with their wives in the Maine woods.

Bangor (Me.) *News*

Last year he paddled up and down the De Soto pool for five continuous hours and has been swimming steadily ever since.

Savannah (Ga.) *Evening Press*

St. Paul's Episcopal Church was destroyed by fire today with help from Bridgewater, West Bridgewater, Stoughton and Rockland.

Malden (Mass.) *News*

The board reached a final decision regarding uniforms. The tourists will simply wear uniform gray hats with a Tulsa hatband and carry canes.

Tulsa (Okla.) *Daily World*

Penny is now attending university at Kent, Ohio, having been driven out by her parents.

Bethesda (Md.) *Bethesda-Chevy Chase Tribune*

An alert young copyreader knows grammer.

New York (N.Y.) *Editor & Publisher*

Her slim figure swayed with the rhythm of the music that she lifted slightly and her white lids drew from the instrument, her chin closed over her china blue eyes.

Los Angeles (Calif.) *Record*

"It is safer to fly in winter than in summer," Mr. Taylor pointed out today. "In cases of forced landings, many friends which can not be used in summer because of water and mud are frozen in the winter and make first class landing places."

Watertown (N.Y.) *Daily Standard*

Local dealers make it plain that there is no obligation when you go to their showroom. They want you to come as their guests, feel free to ask all the questions you care to, and enjoy yourself 10 percent.

Cherokee (Iowa) *Courier*

Saunderson has occasionally been seen shopping and lurching in New York with his future bride.

New York (N.Y.) *Daily News*

From Llandrindrod you proceed along the lovely valley of the Ithon, growing more beautiful as you proceed.

Boston (Mass.) *Traveler*

She took refuse in an abandoned lookout atop the mountain.

Bellingham (Wash.) *Herald*

Their arms hang listlessly from their shoulders, when they are at ease, and the long, strong hands dangle straight to the ground.

Portland (Me.) *Press Herald*

It's important to apply a goo night cream before retiring.

Milwaukee (Wisc.) *Journal*

Mrs. Jennings, twenty-eight, is 5 feet 9½ inches tall, weighs 135 pounds and has a thirty-five-inch bust twenty-five-inch waist and thirty-sex-inch hips.

New York (N.Y.) *Herald Tribune*

You may develop a scrawny neck by exercising. Stand with feet about eighteen inches apart, body erect, chin in; without moving the body turn head sharply to the right three times, then to the left.

Chicago (Ill.) *Tribune*

Princess Margaret, looking fit and relaxed, returned from Ireland with her husband, Lord Snowdon, who failed to mar her holiday.

San Francisco (Calif.) *Examiner*

The barges capsized while being tossed from Haverstraw to New York City.

Poughkeepsie (N.Y.) *Journal*

No trouble to shipping was reported, although ten vessels had been sunk or damaged.

Portland (Ore.) *Oregonian*

The farmer is prepared to stand on his own feet but has to be properly financed to do this.

Ridgetown (Canada) *Dominion*

The Home Bureau held its annual picnic last Thursday. No program was planned so the group talked about members who were not present.

Tuscola (Ill.) *Review*

She was a starlet away back in the early 30s when she was in her early thirsties.

Los Angeles (Calif.) *Mirror-News*

In the automobile accident Miss Susan Barker received multiple lacerations, hemorrhage and acute alcoholism.

Winter Haven (Fla.) *News-Chief*

Rogers Hornsby, the St. Louis star, won the 1920 betting championship of the National League.

St. Louis (Mo.) *Globe-Democrat*

While trimming a cottonwood tree Monday, M. T. Cummings suffered a severe blow on his head when a large branch turned and struck him.

Omaha (Nebr.) *World Herald*

I dropped the receiver out of my hand and almost knocked out a front toot.

Norfolk (Va.) *Virginian-Pilot*

Mrs. Carl Wiggins, the dietician, stated that the best way to lose weight was to dance on an empty stomach.

Kansas City (Mo.) *Star*

Mrs. William Laurence has been entertaining a large group of relatives from a distance the past several weeks.

Ludington (Mich.) *News*

Marjorie Evans, a cashier at the bank, was slightly bruised Monday afternoon when the car driven by George Baker struck her in front of the bank. Mr. Baker is to be commended for the consideration he showed for Miss Evans. He stopped the car immediately, picking her up and feeling her all over to make sure no bones were broken, after which he insisted on taking her home where he could make a closer examination. We are glad to hear that outside of a bruised hip she escaped injury.

Norwood (Ohio) *Enterprise*

Seaman First Class Marvin Schane is home for a short visit. He says that since enlisting in the Navy he has spent a lot of time loving it up in all parts of the world.

Fort Smith (Ark.) *Southwest American*

Mr. Robert Carlson stood third in milk and butter-fat production, having an average of 542 pounds of milk and 26.1 pounds of butter-fat.

Boulder (Colo.) *Camera*

The bandits demanded heavy ransom for their release, threatening to cut off their heads and then put them to death if the money was not forthcoming.

Pasadena (Calif.) *Independent*

The engagement of Miss Finkleson was announced by the bride-elect's mother. Yes, there she was, still propped up in the garage. Mr. Smith gladly donated her to the Mariner's Museum, and Mr. Jones restored her to her former beauty.

Jacksonville (Fla.) *Times-Union*

Jack Quinn, veteran football pitcher, today was signed by the Cincinnati Reds.

Amarillo (Tex.) *Globe-News*

Never throw away bones left from a roast or shoulder. Put them on in cold water, and if cooked several hours a very good soap may be obtained with the addition of diced vegetables.

Louisville (Ky.) *Courier-Journal*

Mrs. Welliver is enjoying a visit with her mother. She says she may stall all winter.

Marion (Mich.) *Press*

George Clelland is suffering from a severe catch in his back which he sustained while lifting a tub of water. George had the tub lifted up in midair when a catch in his back would permit him to neither put the tub down or raise it higher and ever since he has not been able to straighten up.

Santa Ana (Calif.) *Register*

Professor McLennan, in discussing the possibility of producing helium from the gas and oil fields of Alberta, says this non-inflammable gas is now being burned daily in Calgary stoves.

Winnipeg (Canada) *Free Press Evening Bulletin*

When telephone directors become obsolete, they are usually gathered and sold to wastepaper companies for conversion into pulp and the manufacture of new paper. They are torn in two lengthwise, then chopped into small bits in a powerful machine.

Boston (Mass.) *Traveler*

The bride is to be resurfaced with brick, laid herringbone style on a bed of sand with concrete mixture poured in the joints.

Wilmington (Del.) *News*

Picking up his hammer and the two broads he started back in the cabin to finish his job.

Muskogee (Okla.) *Phoenix*

The Hawkins Real Estate Company sold the old Burnaby mansion for $75,000 last week. This is the highest price ever paid for a mouse in Crawford County.

Van Buren (Ark.) *Courier*

Are you certain that your milk comes from disease-free crows?

New Britain (Conn.) *Daily Herald*

The Navy Department announced late Thursday that Midshipman Earl Blair Zirkle of Kansas, who declined to accept his commission recently, has changed his mind, and Secretary Wilbur has directed the super-intendent of the Naval Academy at Annapolis to swear.

Milwaukee (Wisc.) *Sentinel*

After giving the question considerable consideration, Safety Director Wilkins made the following statement: "If all the people driving automobiles would stay home, traffic accidents would drop drastically."

Little Rock (Ark.) *Democrat*

Mrs. Marge Bowder slipped in her garage and struck an apple box. She incurred injury to her ribs which was very painful and also where she landed.

Keizer (Ore.) *News*

Mrs. Leroy Gibson has returned after spending two weeks in Chicago mixing religion with pleasure.

Muncie (Ind.) *Church Bulletin*

The recent earthquake in northern California has in-creased the attendance of the First Baptist church over 200%.

Roseville (Calif.) *Church Bulletin*

Two other shots rang out, one of which pierced the slain man in the forehead, causing instant death.

Helena (Mont.) *Independent*

"I don't know why I'm hitting better this year," said Groat. "I just keep swigging away and a few more base hits have been falling in on me."

Los Angeles (Calif.) *Times*

25

To the surprise of Mr. and Mrs. W. G. Baker, they are enjoying a family reunion.

Bartlesville (Okla.) *Examiner-Enterprise*

The rebels stood at attention . . . their arms were stacked in a corner of the ship's saloon.

Bangor (Me.) *News*

Industrial Boulevard is empty because it is a road to nowhere. Work is underway to extend it.

San Leandro (Calif.) *News*

Linn county is getting ready to eradicate cattle and thereby insure good, safe, clean milk and pure beef.

Cedar Rapids (Iowa) *Marion Gazette*

Rudy Vallee, crooner and orchestra leader, was shaken and bruised today when his car left the road and overturned during a storm. It was feared his vocal cords were not injured.

San Luis Obispo (Calif.) *Telegram-Tribune*

The whole property reeks of gentile poverty.

New York (N.Y.) *World-Telegram*

Due to the cooperation and generosity of Petersburg firms and individuals about $1,000 worth of improvements have been achieved for only $8,000.

Petersburg (Va.) *Progress-Index*

Although there are no horses in the U. S. Naval Academy, Capt. Wilson, athletic officer, has one hanging over his door for good luck.

Chattanooga (Tenn.) *News-Free Press*

The Society for Pure English offers this dialog as a warning against the careless use of prepositions:

Sick Child: "I want to be read to."

Nurse: "What book do you want to be read to out of?"

Sick Child: "Robinson Crusoe."

Nurse goes out and returns with "The Swiss Family Robinson."

Sick Child: "What did you bring me that book to be read to out of from for?"

Chicago (Ill.) *Christian Advocate*

One of the best places in town to have a large dinner party is the home of Mr. and Mrs. D. V. Jennings on Portland Heights.

Portland (Ore.) *Reporter*

Grease new twins thoroughly and bake them slowly in an oven for an hour or so before using. They will not stick so easily.

Albany (N.Y.) *Knickerbocker Press*

Although the wind subsided and calm reigned for a while during the evening, guests were blowing from nearly all directions at midnight.

Boise (Idaho) *Statesman*

The passing of Mr. McDougall is requested by his host of friends.

Wilmington (Del.) *Journal*

The Government unveiled its new income tax forms, including a simple 15-lie card for wage earners.

Galveston (Tex.) *News*

There are certain rules and regulations that apply in forming a 4-H club. First, the chief requisite is to have an adult leader, like myself, which can be a man or woman or a combination of both.

Van Buren (Ark.) *Press Argus*

A dispatch from Moorehead, Minn., said Red River Valley farmers will love heavily because of potatoes damaged by freezing in the fields.

Minneapolis (Minn.) *Journal*

The French Line S. S. *San Diego* arrived Saturday with California passengers and European frights.

Vancouver (Canada) *Province*

He got up, dressed and took a shower.

Chicago (Ill.) *Tribune*

While some came in Tuxedos others walked.

Newark (N.J.) *Star-Ledger*

He pointed out that Colorado's wildlife conservation officers have done effective work in the appreciation of cattle rustlers.

Leadville (Colo.) *Herald Democrat*

Daniel Martin, who lives on East Fiftieth street, was only signed on the back of his head.

Kansas City (Kan.) *Kansan*

Twice on the way across the choppy course he was seized by cramps. Each time he floated and succeeded in kicking them nine miles.

Philadelphia (Pa.) *Public Ledger*

Harper Holt entertained friends from Washington at his New Fane, Vt., farm. Following a hunting expedition for pheasant and quail, Mr. Holt and his guests enjoyed a roast ham dinner.

Greenwich Village (N.Y.) *Villager*

She was questioned in connection with the slaying of a playbody dress manufacturer.

Lancaster (Pa.) *New Era*

Mr. and Mrs. Morrison announce the betrayal of their daughter Wanda.

Brooklyn (N.Y.) *Eagle*

On July 11th, he suffered a stroke but with the loving care of his family and his kind and efficient nurse, he never fully recovered.

Platteville (Wisc.) *Journal*

Two women were held up and robbed and a third succeeded in beating off her assailant over the weekend.

Dallas (Tex.) *Times Herald*

The defendant resumed his seat and watched the jury with his dark eyes, set between a thin Roman nose.

Kansas City (Mo.) *Times*

Friends of Mr. and Mrs. Fred Wilkerson are parents of a seven and a half pound baby boy born last week.

Oroville (Calif.) *Mercury-Register*

Of late he has taken a deep interest in religion and this, together with his love of the great outdoors, has endeared him in the hearts of the community. It was no unusual sight to see him standing on the church steps, drinking in the sun, hatless and coatless, in all kinds of weather.

Pomeroy (Ohio) *Democrat*

The two highway engineers examined the bride very carefully, using a blowtorch to clear away underbrush as they looked underneath. They were of one opinion, a new paint job would help.

Little Rock (Ark.) *Democrat*

The charming nine-room brick building was designed by the late Phillip Newton, whose exterior suggested spacious comfort within.

Denver (Colo.) *Rocky Mountain News*

Mrs. Frank Norton, the very proud mother of a baby daughter, has returned from the hospital. The boy and mother and father are getting along fine.

Portland (Ore.) *Oregonian*

All during the testimony he hardly moved in his chair. For most of the time he rested his head on his chin.

Fort Worth (Tex.) *Star-Telegram*

Miss Ayre's winter ice-box which she keeps on the back porch had been carried down the alley, but since there had been nothing in it, its contents were undisturbed.

Roanoke (Va.) *Times*

Reverend Henry Rogers is now pastoring in Brooklyn.

Newark (N.J.) *Church Bulletin*

At the hospital, Mrs. Robinson explained that she stepped on a piece of soap and skidded right out the window. Her only injury was a wrecked etaoin etaoin

Beckley (W. Va.) *Post-Herald*

The race will start and finish at the Elk's Club at 8:30 o'clock in the morning.

Long Branch (N.J.) *Record*

Arthur Morrison was seriously burned Saturday afternoon when he came in contact with a high voltage wife.

Albuquerque (N.M.) *Tribune*

Al Hubel and his son Cleo, farmers near here, are sharpshooters extraordinary. They have bagged 510 cows during the last year, collecting the county bounty of 10 cents on each—or a total of $51.

San Francisco (Calif.) *Examiner*

Fair Board members and friends are to have a "work night" on Thursday. Those participating are urged to wear clothes and bring tools.

Sandusky (Ohio) *Register*

Calvin P. Foulke, of Whitemarsh, won two distinctions at the annual class elections of the seniors of Princeton. He was voted the "most likely bachelor" and the "greatest woman heater."

Morristown (Pa.) *Register*

The girls speak English very well, to have been in the USA only since June, but you have to listen very carefully to understand them, for they speak very fast rnplvcaweesaunelileiooooobelio.

Cleveland (Ohio) *Herald*

108 of last year's high school graduates were married, this involved 89 girls and 19 boys.

Evansville (Pa.) *Press*

She made the statement as she received the Woman of the Rear Award.

New York (N.Y.) *Daily News*

The sewing circle has invited the Matrons Club to attend its May 3 tea, to be held in Bruce Hall at 2 p.m. Miss Polly Hitchcock will take on the Hebrides Island.

Cape Cod (Mass.) *Standard-Times*

Nudism would be bared in Michigan under a bill introduced in the house Wednesday.

Kalamazoo (Mich.) *Gazette*

American air mail contracts will be awarded only to American companies using American equipment and American crows.

Twin Falls (Idaho) *Times-News*

Turning a knob on a new kitchen table swings out a lower shelf to enable a person to walk while seated on a chair.

Martinez (Calif.) *Morning News Gazette*

The Young Matrons Bridge Club met Saturday night at the home of Mrs. T. J. Lloyd. No prizes were given because none of the members knew how to keep score. It is hoped that this situation will soon be corrected.
— Le Center (Minn.) *Leader*

It is permissible to spank a child if one has a definite end in view.
Tulsa (Okla.) *World*

Kenneth P. Lord returned to the tire division last year. He was born in Washington with a bachelor degree in accounting.
Huntington Park (Calif.) *Signal*

Seen on the lawn of Mr. and Mrs. Bobby Long Sunday; a car with a Tennessee hag.
Calhoun City (Miss.) *Monitor-Herald*

Locally the Shrine Clothing Fund gives complete outfits to between 125 and 150 children to indignant families each Christmas.
El Paso (Tex.) *Times*

Winnipeg needs a completed TV network, so that viewers can get live TV from hither and yawn.
Winnipeg (Canada) *Tribune*

Patty Piellusch celebrated her sixth birthday with a party in her home. There were ten litter guests.
Little Neck (N.Y.) *Ledger*

No other trains run so far for so long a distance as the "Florida Special."

Boston (Mass.) Record American

She appealed to me and I guess $ appealed to her.

Boston (Mass.) Traveler

He was the pride and job of his mother's heart.

Willimantic (Conn.) Daily Chronicle

The vicechairman of the board, who is fairly bald, countered that he did not think there was anything wrong with bears, and added: "I've been thinking about growing one on top of my head."

St. Louis (Mo.) Post-Dispatch

She lives with her brother, a blue parakeet, a white poodle and a television set in her fireplace.

Redwood City (Calif.) Tribune

Just one last visit to the "Old Kentucky Home" and then Miss Virginia Norton is going back to the colorful romance of the Orient, and to the uniformed romance of the American naval officers to whom she is engaged.

San Francisco (Calif.) Examiner

Alice Wallington has been engaged as stewardess and social hostess aboard the S. S. *Alexandria,* which sails tomorrow. Before leaving port she will have her barnacles scraped.

Boston (Mass.) Herald

Hazel Brannon Smith writes in her Lexington (Miss.) Advertiser about a mechanical hoe that has

34

been invented by H. H. Peterman of Holmes County. She suggests that this hoe which is simply hitched on a tractor may revolutionize cotton growing. The things that discouraged me most in farming, as I look back on it, were milking and hoeing. With a mechanical milker and hoer farming should not be too arduous.

Gulfport (Miss.) *Dixie Guide*

Until he recovers, the Crown Prince will carry on with the royal cuties.

(New York, N.Y.) Associated Press

Early yellow peaches and apples are being marketed by local fruit growers. oGod prices are being received, farmers said.

Hartford (Conn.) *Times*

Many officers and their waves from the Bremerton Navy Yard are planning to attend the theater this evening.

Seattle (Wash.) *Times*

Relatively "good" ages seem to alternate as the child grows older with "bad" ages. Thus 2½ years of age tends to be a rather bad age. Things usually improve markedly around 30.

Portland (Ore.) *Journal*

Henry Moser is planning the construction of a hothouse, wherein it is planned to raise avocados and guano, and other tropical fruits and plants.

Monterey (Calif.) *County Post*

Social Security administrators are having trouble explaining this advice issued by one of their regional offices: "If you should die or retire after June 30, 1952, get in touch with your Social Security Office."

New York (N.Y.) *Newsweek*

Mrs. Doebler then gave a brief biological sketch of her parents' 50 years together.

Kenyon (Minn.) *Leader*

Mr. Jim Watson, for more than fifty years a citizen of Sulphur Springs, did eat his home Wednesday afternoon.

Dallas (Tex.) *News*

A southwest wind blew at eight miles an hour from the northeast Tuesday.

Erie (Pa.) *Times*

At Beebe, Ark., Mrs. Sally Hill twisted her home from its foundations and in Jonesboro, Ark., winds, which reached 80 miles-an-hour, caused minor property damage.

Muskogee (Okla.) *Phoenix*

Secretary of State Barrows announced plans for an outdoor billboard advertising campaign against carless automobile drivers.

Augusta (Me.) *Kennebec Journal*

City ambulance surgeon called to city ambulance surgeon at 7 o'clock this morning to treat a man who smashed a nose after practically demolishing his car by ramming it in the rear end while in a drowsy condition after driving all night from New Hampshire in broad daylight on Fairfield avenue.

Bridgeport (Conn.) *Post*

Kyle Wagg who has been suffering from a badly infected hand for several weeks is much improved this week. He mashed his finger with a hammer which grew worse.

Pateros (Wash.) *News*

Both candidates for Sheriff are well liked and long time residents of the city. If you wish to be arrested in a courteous, efficient manner, either of the gentlemen should be able to give complete satisfaction.

Tacoma (Wash.) *News Tribune*

Wednesday afternoon the hospital alumnae association entertained the girls at a chicken barbecue at Perry Lake, Cave Spring. The chickens were cooked to a delicious turn, on a girl, by the lake.

Rome (Ga.) *News-Tribune*

Mallon unloosed a pig which hit Bucci, the initial clubber, but the player remained at first.

White Plains (N.Y.) *Reporter Dispatch*

At a Red Cross meeting in Washington a chairman was giving his workers a pep talk: "I know you are tired. But many of our greatest men were tired—and they carried on. Take General Marshall, for instance. He is carrying on—although all he wants to do is retire to his estate in Virginia with Mrs. Eisenhower."

New York (N.Y.) *King Features*

Her death followed a lingering illness that had made her an individual for several years.

Akron (Ohio) *Beacon Journal*

Col. Arthur F. Foran, controller of the Port of New York, was charged with failure to prevent liquor smuggling by the New Jersey Anti-Saloon League head.

Danbury (Conn.) *Evening News*

A Standard Oil Co. employee was in Spring Valley last week decorating the widows of the various business firms, who are handling the Orinate products.

Spring Valley (Minn.) *Tribune*

The Orpheons were entertained at their Feb. 17 meeting by an accordian solo by Mary Jane Phelps. Roma Leichner played a piano solo and Gloria McKim sang a solo.

The members decided to have outside entertainment.

Cleveland (Ohio) *Plain Dealer*

Miss Hilda May Gordon, the first woman to travel round the world on her paint brush.

Belfast (Ireland) *Belfast News Letter*

Wednesday night Miss Gail Malcom and Miss Gail Prather gave "The Light Allevidles the Darkness of Suffering." Thursday night was postponed until a later date.

Walton (Ga.) *Tribune*

The carnival, located at the Hun School, will feature nine booths ranging from sponge throwing to daughter of Dr. Alfred S. Cook, donated by the campers to be used as prizes and all proceeds are donated to Liberia.

Princeton (N.J.) *Packet*

Cocktail dresses in pastels or vivid prints will be seen frightening up the landscape in resorts and clubs these summer evenings.

Eugene (Ore.) *Register-Guard*

Majority of the 37 graduates plan to enter teaching. Seven will be married this summer. Four are graduate nurses. Three will attend the music camp at Interlocken, Mich. Three of the graduates plan to enter the field of dietetics. Six will teach. The rest will work.

Baltimore (Md.) *Sun*

The Peakcock skirt, created so that a hostess won't trip over her skirt while running to greet cocktails or pour out guests . . .

Miami (Fla.) *Daily News*

She was as pretty as a picture, and wrapped about her throat was an antique gold chair.

Salt Lake City (Utah) *Telegram*

The ranch house of the Ralph McGlockin place between State Bridge and Wolcott was entirely destroyed by fire last week. For twenty-five days it has been one of the landmarks of the country.

Craig (Colo.) *Empire*

Weerts, whose parents have moved to Davenport, Ia., was second in the high hurdles and third in the low hurdles. Peart was third in the hospital.

La Salle (Ill.) *News-Tribune*

There will be no open season on prairie chickens and the season on all other upland game girls is closed.

Portland (Ore.) *Journal*

Fourteen Socialists, arrested for pocketing theatres, are scheduled to face disorderly conduct charges Friday.

New York (N.Y.) *Sun*

Apparently misled by appearances, six-armed hijackers today held up Edward Hughes of Garfield.

Los Angeles (Calif.) *Times*

The booze was found to contain only 44 percent alcohol and 66 percent formaldehyde.

Memphis (Tenn.) *Commercial Appeal*

Miss Nellie Gregory has returned to her home on Federal Street after an extended say with friends in Nelson County.

Lynchburg (Va.) *News*

Thomas P. Gore, formerly Senator from Oklahoma, is back from abroad, having fulfilled a boyhood ambition. In Rome he stood where Mary Anthony did and declaimed: "Friends, Romans, Countrymen."

Rochester (N.Y.) *Democrat and Chronicle*

Dear Editor: Please send us your June 14th Sunday supplement of "Travel in Arkansas" and things to do. We expect to visit your wonderful state this summer. We intend to camp out and have three children.

Little Rock (Ark.) *Democrat*

Mr. and Mrs. Gregory, Mr. Carl Williams and Miss Thelma Clark were visitors at the fair last week. The three harried people and Miss Clark enjoyed it very much.

Des Moines (Iowa) *Tribune*

Official announcement was made today of the approaching marriage of Prince Takamatsu, younger brother of the Emperor, to Kikuko Tokugawa, granddaughter of the last of the Shotguns.

New York (N.Y.) *Times*

Martin, of Brewster, who has been in a New York hospital for two months with puss on the knee, will spend a month with his sister, Mrs. LeRoy McMullins.

Somers-Salem (N.Y.) *Press*

To the sheriffs and cow-punchers, the robbery recalled memories of "Bill" Carlisle, who, single-handed, held up three Union Pacific passenger trains in 1813 and later, escaped from prison to rob another in 1920.

Memphis (Tenn.) *Commercial-Appeal*

Dunn told police he had installed the alarm following several raids on his chicken cook.

Rochester (N.Y.) *Democrat and Chronicle*

Mr. Charles Simmonds is considered by many one of New Jersey's lawyers.

Princeton (N.J.) *Packet*

A son was born to Mr. and Mrs. John Phillips, general delivery.

Benton Harbor (Mich.) *News Palladium*

The bride is approximately eighteen feet wide from buttress to buttress.

Kansas City (Mo.) *Star*

The cast of characters, local talent, performed with credit and each member electrocuted their part perfectly.

Harlem (Ga.) *Columbia News*

The plan would curb marketing of milk by 15 percent. It would distribute some milk to underfed city children, kill deceased cows, and redistribute healthy cows to needy farmers.

Longview (Wash.) *News*

While this was a contest among grammar-school boys, parents had a hand in it also. In most cases, when a parent was present, it was either the father or mother.

Upland (Calif.) *News*

Mrs. Newton occasioned a lot of interest by wearing her back suspended from her waist at the back.

Los Angeles (Calif.) *Herald-Examiner*

Lovers of fine old furniture, quaint heirlooms, beautiful glassware and china and rare tapestries and linens would have a field day examining his trousers.

Birmingham (Ala.) *Post*

Bathers sought refuge away from the fire on the wet side of the lake.

Syracuse (N.Y.) *Herald-Journal*

Horton's throw bettered by three and four-quarters inches the previous record.

Port Arthur (Tex.) *News*

Sixteen Ohio hunters died of gunshot wounds during 1951, the Ohio Division of Wildfire reported.

Akron (Ohio) *Beacon Journal*

Policeman Leo Grant was shot through the stomache and John Marcinoak, Indiana Harbor taxicab-driver, through the hip, while a trusty at the jail was shot in the excitement.

San Francisco (Calif.) *Call-Bulletin*

Mrs. Horace Sumner is visiting her husband Mr. Bart Humphrey in Dallas this week-end.

Waco (Tex.) *Times-Herald*

Mr. and Mrs. Horace Creswell, of Tennessee, are seeing their loved ones here. Dr. C. H. Workman removed Mr. Creswell's tonsils and they are now with his sister, Mrs. Palmer.

Greenwood (S.C.) *Index Journal*

The bedding will take place in Paris in July.
Stamford (Conn.) Advocate

Governor Fuller Warren of Florida went back to the hospital, where he is recovering from "physical and nervous exhaustion" after spending Christmas with his family.
Little Rock (Ark.) Gazette

Flourishing their revolvers and hurling threatening epitaphs at their victims the bandits herded them together behind a prescription counter.
Joliet (Ill.) Herald-News

The defendant had been charged with wreckless driving and failure to heed a stop sign. He was found not guilty of the wreckless driving charge.
Lawrence (Kan.) Journal-World

He was born in Bristol and prior to that he was employed by the American Silver Co.
Hartford (Conn.) Courant

Born, December 17, to Mr. and Mrs. Harold Lanning of College Avenue, a son. Answered Three Alarms.
Adrian (Mich.) Daily Telegram

Mrs. Cora May Walker has recently been placed on the shelves of the Chelsea Public Library.
Burlington (Vt.) Free Press

In Tuesday's Newsday, what was intended as the last paragraph of an article by Dr. Sheldon Weiss supporting fluoridation appeared, instead, as the first paragraph of an article by Dr. A. A. London opposing fluoridation. Although the main import of these two significant articles remained intact, Newsday regrets the error.

New York (N.Y.) *Newsday*

The male chorus sang several songs, before and with a piano solo by George Anson. Both were given generous applesauce.

Bloomington (Ill.) *Pantagraph*

A silver tea for the members of the Wet End Women's Christian Temperance Union was given Tuesday.

Binghamton (N.Y.) *Press*

He was carried to the hospital where his condition was pronounced as undetermined. He was held for further observation and later it was found that he was dead.

Muskogee (Okla.) *Phoenix*

Town officials are up in arms over the wanton vandalism of one of the flower pots on the Washington Avenue bridge.

Pulaski (Va.) *Southwest Times*

The city administration has laid out plans for a better zoo, with barless cages, a special enclosure for children, and other improvements.

Denver (Colo.) *Rocky Mountain News*

The Mets won the last game of the double-header from the Cardinals. They now have a one game streak going.

St. Louis (Mo.) *Post-Dispatch*

Cold cut meat sandwiches are on the menu, in addition to the usual foul course meats in the restaurant.

West Warwick (R.I.) *Pawtuxet Valley Times*

Samuel Angelo injured the big toe on his left front foot when the foot became entangled in the blades of a power lawn mower.

Newark (N.J.) *Evening News*

The driver reported that he lost control of the bus in an effort to keep hitting an automobile on which he saw a front tire blow out.

El Paso (Tex.) *Times*

A Pasadena man 84 years old has just barked upon his fourth marriage.

Pasadena (Calif.) *Star-News*

Dear Miss Dix:
My husband and I have been married for nearly two weeks. How long will it be before I get pregnant?

Chicago (Ill.) *Herald & Examiner*

The incident at the jail caused the sheriff to order his men to check their shacking equipment for defects.

Hartford (Conn.) *Times*

"I didn't get hurt at all," she explained, as one of the nurses smeared a deep red mendicant over her knees.

Minneapolis (Minn.) *Tribune*

Sheriff Herb Person was called by a motorist who reported seeing a deer run from the road into a field.

The sheriff jumped into his can and answered the call, two miles northwest of Columbus.

Omaha (Nebr.) *World-Herald*

It has been officially reported that the Germans have taken Castoria.

(New York, N.Y.) United Press

Latrobe's annual Pageant of Drum and Bulge Corps here Saturday is attracting one Canadian entry.

Pittsburgh (Pa.) *Post-Gazette & Sun Telegraph*

Immediately after the ceremony, Mr. and Mrs. Duck left for a wading trip to points in the Smoky Mountains.

Texarkana (Tex.) *Daily News*

Dwyer, in high spirits and smiling broadly, said he felt "wonderful to be leaving the prison." He was clad in a brown and green and white polka-dot necktie.

New York (N.Y.) *Journal-American*

Leon weighed nine pounds, 11 ouches.

Grand Forks (N.D.) *Herald*

What's more, she said, she wouldn't mind marrying a baldy, wouldn't mind marrying a baldy, the 10 most interesting bald-headed men.

Fort Worth (Tex.) *Star-Telegram*

"These are still difficult days for the retail trade," said Mr. Hobbs, salesmanager, to the group of new salesmen, "and in all your dealings with prospective

47

buyers remember that old adage, the customer is always tight."

Denver (Colo.) Post

The installation of two-way radio by the police will make it more difficult for justice to escape the clutches of the law here than ever before.

Brazil (Ind.) Daily Times

Columbia Records and its record-smashing Record of the Month Club have the display windows in the old Orpheum Theater building this week.

Terre Haute (Ind.) Tribune

The wedding was an event of 2 p.m. Dec. 24 in Our Saviors rhinestone trimmed jacket. Mrs. William Dueber was the matron of honor and she wore a Evangelical Lutheran Church, San Diego, Calif.

Neosha (Mo.) News

After each rush hour ride, printed cards will be passed out to all patrons to get their reactions. They can check one of the printed replies on the front— or just write how they feel on the back side.

Boston (Mass.) Globe

She left all her fathers at home except a pink one that peeked out from under the folds of her hat.

Los Angeles (Calif.) Evening News

Twenty-four students from Newport News are among the 125 Virgins enrolled in the freshman class.

Newport News (Va.) Daily Press

The bride wore a white satin gown with sweetheart neckline and long sleeves which ended in a joint over her head.

Freeman (S.D.) *Courier*

Both teams lost to Shoshone by one pint. The Panthers-Shoshone score was 10-9, the Rattlers-Shoshone 9-8.

Barstow (Calif.) *Desert Dispatch*

An eight-hour day and one day's rest out of seven for state police is provided for in a bill introduced by Senator three sisters. Funeral service will be held on Thursday.

Kingston (N.J.) *Freeman*

The pastor will preach his farewell address. The choir will sing "Break Forth Into Joy."

Lewiston (Idaho) *Morning Tribune*

Celia Villa, daughter of Pancho Villa, Mexican revolutionary, and Fred Datig, movie casting director, were married Monday, his studio said, temperatures range as high as 160 degrees.

Reno (Nev.) *Gazette*

The wet and rather cold weather that they had obtained here during the training period undoubtedly has set back some of them. The spinsters, particularly, have not been able to let out as they would like to.

New York (N.Y.) *Times*

Mr. and Mrs. Henry Jensen entertained at Christmas Sunday, Mrs. N. P. Jensen and Will Jensen, Mr. and

Mrs. Sam Carusi and children, and Mr. and Mrs. Will Berry and a recent appendicitis operation.

Fowlerville (Mich.) *Review*

Spokesmen for the congregation say he was very well received and they feel most unfortunate to have him back.

Laredo (Tex.) *Times*

Mr. and Mrs. John Biekri of Watertown, Wisc., spent the week there at their home.

Richmond (Ill.) *Gazette*

Post office technicians have developed new equipment they hope will lease the aching backs of mail handlers.

Buffalo (N.Y.) *Courier-Express*

A young college student walked shivering into a hunting camp today, cold but otherwise in good condition, following a frigid night holed up in a cafe after he became lost while hunting.

Charleston (W. Va.) *Daily Mail*

A farewell banquet was tendered last evening to Wilfred Smith, who leaves with the next group of selectees to be inducted into the Army ... Several brief talks were given and Mr. Smith was presented a small nurse.

Glens Falls (N.Y.) *Times*

Dear Miss Dix:
So many wonderful and exciting things have happened to me since I last wrote you. I've had all my teeth pulled and a new stove and refrigerator put in.

Fort Worth (Tex.) *Star-Telegram*

Mr. LaFavre, manager of the largest bookstore in Niagara Falls stated that honeymooners bought few books or magazines, so few, in fact, that he sometimes wondered what they did for amusement.

New York (N.Y.) *Sun*

For the first time in this war the title of Hero of the Soviet Union was awarded today by the presidium of the Supreme Soviet to a woman flyer. She was decorated with 21 Air force commanders.

St. Louis (Mo.) *Globe-Democrat*

We would walk out to the area where the animals roam free and talk for hours.

Rochester (N.Y.) *Times Union*

The Youth Fellowship met Sunday night with 15 attending. A round table discussion on "Evangelism" was held. For entertainment they wet on a "Jalopy Raid."

Dover (Ohio) *Reporter*

The cost of building an electrically-heated home is lower because there is no need of a furnace and accessory pipelines and cuts. Unless a fireplace is wanted, a chimney is unnecessary too. Elimination of these as well as fuel storage space not only saves construction costs but provides more loving space in the home.

Bridgeport (Conn.) *Sunday Herald*

The new Alec Guiness comedy in which he plays a sailor with a girl in two parts.

Boston (Mass.) *Traveler*

At the close of his address the Senator introduced an old fiend, Lee Leichlighter.

Boise (Idaho) *Statesman*

Patrolman Martin at first looked skeptical, had a look for himself, and talked the thing over with a red police truck.

Easton (Pa.) *Express*

Let a young woman think twice before assuming that a young aspirant for commercial achievement is going to have easy sailing if he marries her own successful father.

Oklahoma City (Okla.) *Oklahoman*

Mr. and Mrs. E. L. Parker of Main Street, parents of daughter born at Wing Memorial under auspices of Universalist Mens Club.

Palmer (Mass.) *Journal Register*

Probably one of the best points about the new car is that it hardly resembles a Hudson except for one section of the grill.

Clarksdale (Miss.) *Daily Press*

She wanted a painting of a robin on a twig, with breast matching the paper. For a model, she sent in a stuffed friend gone south for the last time.

Halifax (Canada) *Mail-Star*

Still a mystery to police is how the money disappeared from the safe. Two boys are required to open the safe.

One is kept at the station and the other is carried by the station manager.

St. Joseph (Mo.) *Gazette*

Joyce Miller, a pupil of Mary Megert Dance Studio, appeared in a dance routine resented by the pupils in a program at the Homecoming.

Girard (Ohio) *News*

The war's biggest thrill for a civilian came today to Mrs. Mildred Batten Hochadel, Prindle Street, wife of a Thunderbolt fighter plane who had been reported missing in action.

Sharon (Pa.) *Herald*

A son belonging to Clarence Gracey of Lyndonville last week gave birth to 20 pigs.

Albion (N.Y.) *Orleans*

Miss L. B. has been ill with a very heavy child for some days.

Jenkintown (Pa.) *Times-Chronicle*

A bunch of smouldering rags was quickly doused by the Washington Hose Company upon their arrival in a bucket of water.

Coatesville (Pa.) *Record*

I remove the bits of dough from my pastry board by sprinkling the board liberally with salt and rubbing it with a damp sloth.

Erie (Pa.) *Morning News*

John Nance Garner fed his chickens, then took a tramp around the garden.

Houston (Tex.) *Press*

Following the funeral service Friday afternoon at the home of Mrs. Tryton, conducted by Rev. Smith, interment was made in Maple Leaf Cemetery. Loss is covered by insurance.

Ottawa (Canada) *Citizen*

The Milton Boob Club will meet Monday night at the home of Mrs. Adolph Oelrichs.

Walla Walla (Wash.) *Union-Bulletin*

The pretty expectant mother was called to the stand by the District Attorney.

Newark (N.J.) *Star-Ledger*

The buried man emerged from his trap near the seaport Gdynia recently with a knee-length beard and hair hanging down to his angles.

Atlantic (Iowa) *News Telegraph*

The man threw his leg over the railing, clambered on top of it and rolled off.

Columbus (Ohio) *State Journal*

Mrs. Elsa Rodeen suffered a painful injury Saturday when she tripped over a rug while moving furniture in the parlor and fell, fracturing her knee-cap and demolishing her whatnot.

McNary (Calif.) *Blade*

Alex Jackson, colored, was chasing a cow about two weeks ago, and he ran off into Tom Jackson's well, also colored.

Louisville (Miss.) *Winston County Journal*

But these words haven't exactly been taken to the hearts and panties of the nation's women.

Amarillo (Tex.) *Times*

In the past, the patrol has concentrated on inspection of school buses as its primary safety 'weapon.' Now, as the school bus drivers' chauffeur licenses expire, the driver will be required to take a re-examination to insure his continued incompetance.

Wheeling (W. Va.) *Intelligencer*

Princess Elizabeth may become a moth again by the end of the year.

Honolulu (Hawaii) *Star-Bulletin*

Mr. Jones was born in Brooklyn and came to the United States 46 years ago.

Long Island (N.Y.) *Daily Press*

Last riots will be held at the home on Saturday afternoon at 2:00 p.m.

Gastonia (Ga.) *Daily Gazette*

If you're wondering about the reason for those shutdowns and slowdowns in war plants, the government's answer is eatoin eatoin

Washington (D.C.) *Wide World Features*

For cleaning soiled wallpaper, take a loaf of ordinary white bread, break off the crust and quickly run up the wall.

Salt Lake City (Utah) *Telegram*

Mrs. Kornberger said that her husband beat her frequently. A divorce was recommended after she testified that she finally left her husband and came here to love.

Philadelphia (Pa.) *Bulletin*

To a citizen like myself who was weaned on home brew during the days of the noble experiment, a trip to Oklahoma is an experience in nostalgia. a5asodg cmfw cmfw

Detroit (Mich.) *Free Press*

The cats farmers managed to get in early, before the rains came, will be all right, he said.

East Palestine (Ohio) *Daily Leader*

Once neighbors helped one another during barn raising and bee husking.

Providence (R.I.) *Journal*

Most men make the mistake of not washing their faces thoroughly with hot soup and water before they begin shaving.

Coatesville (Pa.) *Record*

To keep apples from spoiling, place them in a cold room in a house occupied by eight children.

San Pedro (Calif.) *News-Pilot*

Like most hospitals in the country, today, large or small, it isn't adequately stuffed.

Clarksdale (Miss.) *Daily Press*

Mr. Dreyfuss pointed out that "A bomber going 300 miles an hour at 14,000 feet which aims at Radio City and hits Jersey City will be doing well."

New York (N.Y.) *Herald Tribune*

The Beans furnished music for a few social dances after the meeting.

Lewiston (Me.) *Sun*

Police are attempting to locate Joseph Malcolm Adkins for an important massage.

St. Petersburg (Fla.) *Independent*

This program is brought to you by your neighborhood shoe repairman and O'Sullivan, America's Number 1 heel.

New York (N.Y.) *Daily News*

The nomadic Nunatmiuk eskimos built portable dame-shaped willow huts.

Bedford (Ind.) *Daily Times-Mail*

Pop Pius, tears streaming from his eyes, paid sorrowful tribute to the Polish nation.

Columbus (Ohio) *Citizen*

Marilyn Monroe wore a tight filling dress with a plunging neckline plunging neckline.

Los Angeles (Calif.) *Daily News*

Older people as well as children enjoy Valentine's Day. In fact, I think they like it even more, for they have experienced romance and look back on it through mellowing rind and $1/3$ tsp. nutmeg.

Baltimore (Md.) *News-Post*

A Southern Railway passenger train collided head-on with a friend Thursday.

Muskogee (Okla.) *Daily Phoenix*

The program, originated in 1934, has grown in popularity and is now one of the most insignificant occasions of the college year.

Charleston (S.C.) *Evening Post*

Marv Rickert an obscene outfielder from Milwaukee, who came up to sub for the injured Jeff Heath, broke Feller's no-hitter.

Champaign-Urbana (Ill.) *News-Gazette*

The trip was virtually without incident. The only excitement came when the bus driver questioned whether it was safe to drive over a small bride. He was reassured by a resident.

Cincinnati (Ohio) *Enquirer*

Friday morning road crews began their work covering ashes and cinders with new ice, making traveling more dangerous.

Somerset (Pa.) *American*

Weather Report: Partly cloudy and mild today. 35 Sunday, cloudy followed by night.

Roanoke (Va.) *World-News*

58

The bride graduated from Dexter High School in 1949. She has been worsing in Washington for the F. B. I. during the past two years.

Dexter (Mo.) *Statesman*

Last Spring Baltimore sports editor John F. Steadman said he'd eat his words if the Orioles didn't win the League pennant. Thursday he did. But the job was made more palatable when outfielder Jackie Brandt ran the newspaper column through an electric grinder and mixed it with sirloin, celery stalks and a small union.

Chicago (Ill.) *Daily News*

The A. & P. is actually the Great Atlantic & Pacific Tcat Company.

Columbus (Ohio) *State Journal*

Due to the strike, restaurants scratched milk from their menus.

Greensboro (N.C.) *Daily News*

Sgt. Till of the Women's Army Air Corps will be in Clarksdale to interview any interesting young women.

Clarksdale (Miss.) *Daily Press-Register*

The first event today was the administering of the oats of office to County Judge Milton D. Richardson.

Brownsville (Tex.) *Herald*

Mary Lou had been a good wife to Glen, still their brief marriage had gone on the rocks. Could she have been born under an unlucky star, or was it just fat?

Los Angeles (Calif.) *Herald-Express*

The annual custom of parading the streets until the wee hours of the morning in an assorted array of costumes, making hilarious use of noisemakers and occasionally rubbing soap on store windows when the policemen aren't looking, has become a wartime casualty. Not to mention the harmful pranks that occur when everybody is in bed.

Fort Lauderdale (Fla.) *Daily News*

Tom and Miss Cory were on the teeter-totter board when Miss Cory slipped off and her end flew up resulting in an injury to his vertebrae.

Fresno (Calif.) *Bee*

Police were continuing the thefts today but had no clear picture of their quarry.

Helena (Mont.) *Independent Record*

Cab drivers in Washington even today get a kick out of taking a customer to the White House. One driver cut his feet in half because a newspaper woman gave him the White House address.

Greensburg (Pa.) *Review*

The Sports had lost four straight games and attendance fell off 100% or more.

Fort Worth (Tex.) *Star-Telegram*

If there's anything that can run baseball a close race, as the national sport, it is wimming.

Lincoln (Nebr.) *State Journal*

The bridal couple then passed out and greeted the guests.

Louisville (Ky.) *Courier-Journal*

She wanted a cigarette, so she pulled out a sack of tobacco and began rolling one. That's hard enough to do without a baby on your lap. But with Junior kicking around, the mother got pretty irrigated.

Dallas (Tex.) *News*

Hoping to attract recruits, the Ursuline Convent is opening its doors to girls of 18 and over so they may spend several days sampling the life of the nuts.

Lansing (Mich.) *State Journal*

Wilfrid Blank pleaded guilty in City Magistrate's Court to a charge of housekeeping and was remanded to Tuesday for sentence.

Ottawa (Canada) *Evening Citizen*

In the afternoon all of the tired but happy Joneses sat beneath a huge shade tree and took their time about digesting several tables covered with delicious food.

Manchester (Conn.) *Herald*

Don't worry about children because they skip a meal. Don't tell him stories, don't let him have a toy, don't scold. Remove the fool, go about your business, and let him get hungry for next mealtime.

Seattle (Wash.) *Spokesman-Review*

Howard said the car was a total wreck. Howard said the car was almost a total wreck.

Avenal (Calif.) *Times*

Mrs. Hannah Gabriel who is ill is not so well.

Jamestown (N.Y.) *Post*

Dentist Wilkerson looked into Miss Nichels mouth and could see that the young lady needed braces on her lower teet.

Newark (N.J.) *Star-Eagle*

The bereaved family have lost a good husband, father and grandfather. And we have lost a good friend. But, our loss is His gain; for toward this he had set his hope —"To bet with Christ."

Buffalo Center (Iowa) *Tribune*

The bride was becomingly attired in a street-length lime colored dress of imported linen, offset with a white sequin-trimmed hat and long white gloves. Her shoulder corsage was a large covered reception table, from which coffee and sweet rolls were served.

El Dorado (Kan.) *Times*

The bride was entrancingly gowned in a sheer, soft blue net gown which fell to the floor as she swept down the aisle.

Lamar (Mo.) *Daily Democrat*

The local Salvation Army Red Shield Club living room will have Venetian blonds in every window.

Lewiston (Me.) *Evening Journal*

Another exercise to flatten your stomach is to lie on the floor, tuck your feet under the seat of a chair or couch and in his wife's accomplishments.

Birmingham (Ala.) *News*

Teri-Ann, Cleveland's "blizzard baby," shown above with her mother, Mrs. Harry Zellman, will be two years old Sunday. The child was born in the snow in a hospital parking lot unnoticed by her father and mother, who collapsed as she stepped from an automobile.

Cleveland (Ohio) *Plain Dealer*

Listen to Alice McLane's Fashion Talks
Today's Topic:
    Rise of the one-piece dress
    Every Friday—10:30 a.m.

Salt Lake City (Utah) *Tribune*

Seignon, tall for a Burmese girl, stands five feet six inches tall; waist 22; bust 34. She's in her nylons. Her hips are 35 married.

Minneapolis (Minn.) *Tribune*

The two holdup men were found sleeping nude in the East Saint Louis rooming house. Found on them was the $10,000 taken in the robbery.

St. Louis (Mo.) *Globe Democrat*

Miss Thelma Elmore Jones was married to Bobby Stanley and not Henry Hodges Stanley as was stated in the article on their wedding appearing in a recent edition of the Sun-Journal. The bridegroom's parents are Mr. and Mrs. John B. Stanley and not Mr. and Mrs. H. H. Stanley, as was stated in the same article, and the officiating minister was Rev. E. W. Downing of New Bern and not Rev. A. E. Brown of Bridgeton.

New Bern (N.C.) *Sun-Journal*

Bucky Walters, unwinding after a day of brilliant pitching, fielding and hitting, hopped to his licker and tried to undress with one hand. The other was busy shaking with at least 50 persons.

Tampa (Fla.) *Morning Tribune*

Postmaster Harmon went to Cleveland today for a visit. From there, he will be taken to the Atlanta penitentiary.

Youngstown (Ohio) *Vindicator*

Governor Youngdahl is in Washington today in quest of more Federal hell in repairing flood damage in Minnesota this spring.

(Grand Forks, N.D.) Associated Press

Lloyd said the cold wave would be accompanied by cold weather.

Kansas City (Mo.) *Star*

Roman Catholics and some others went to their churches to have ashes placed in their heads as a symbol of the day.

Athens (Ohio) *Messenger*

Alarmed over the decrease in taxes and population in the County, the council met in emergency session to discuss methods of remedying the situation.

Gloversville (N.Y.) *Morning World*

After every title defense Joe Louis speaks the same words over the radio:

YALE WINS EASTERN TITLE

Dallas (Tex.) *Morning News*

She was a woman in her early thirties, rather well dressed and generally meat in appearance.
Chicago (Ill.) *Christian Advocate*

The Brooklyn bride has more cables on one side than on the other.
Grand Rapids (Mich.) *Press*

The first cars rolled up before the Thirty-Ninth Street entrance about 7:30 o'clock, and it was not until after 9 p.m. that the last of them had entered the opera house.
New York (N.Y.) *Herald-Tribune*

After promising to marry her Miss Duvall alleged young Cory jolted her and wed another.
St. Louis (Mo.) *Post-Dispatch*

On the right is a beautifully curved counter, providing widows for three tellers farther back.
Tacoma (Wash.) *News Tribune*

Population grows at a frightful rate in spite of what the auto drivers can do. We may run out of space in another 100 years. Prof. O'Hare, the staff mathematician, hasn't completed his statistical calculations yet, but he says there'll be at least 40,000 persons to the square meal.

Minneapolis (Minn.) *Tribune*

Mr. and Mrs. Joe Doakes are the parents of a baby girl, following an accident in the apartment.

Oxford (Ohio) *Press*

No man can think and study when he is worn out by pretty things.

Washington (D.C.) *Post*

As she stepped into the hotel lobby the newly-seeded bride was met by several of her college fraternity.

Los Angeles (Calif.) *Daily News*

If you've crickets in your clothes closet or mothers in your mackinaw, you can get 'em to move out.

Pittsburgh (Pa.) *Post-Gazette*

Regular intake of vitamin pills does not assure you of being well-nourished. Vitamin pills are expensive, and they are a poor substitute for ago oddiet.

Lewisburg (Pa.) *Standard-Journal*

The visiting naval officer never was given to vocal volubility. He never did talk much.

Dallas (Tex.) *Times-Herald*

The Civil Aeronautic Authority announced a sentry and a mysterious gunman exchanged shorts Saturday night near the Joliet airport.

Belleville (Ill.) *Daily Advocate*

Mrs. Grace Graham of 2923 Palm Grove Avenue slipped on the floor recently and broke her breast in two places.

Los Angeles (Calif.) *Tribune*

A good housekeeper must be a skilled one. Cooking may be easier nowadays, but it takes a lot of serious stinking and worry to plan, shop for and cook three meals a day.

Seattle (Wash.) *Star*

The coroner's jury, consisting of five men and a woman, rendered its verdict after Mrs. Yoh, wife of Harold L. Yoh, a Philadelphia industrial consultant, reclined to testify.

Coatesville (Pa.) *Record*

Seven Harvard University researchers reported today that a hearing aid can be constructed to work for all dead or hard-of-hearing persons.

(Cambridge, Mass.) United Press

She is cited in Who's Who in America, the International Blue Book (Who's Who in the World), W ho in Education, ho's Who among Women and Lo s ho in Texas.

Austin (Tex.) *American*

A reception followed the ceremony, after which the happy couple left for Vancouver on their honeymoon. On Wednesday they left for Spokane where he is receiving treatment for battle wounds.

Tenino (Wash.) *Independent*

One New York fireman has been killed in the line of duty every seven weeks for the last 35 years.

New York (N.Y.) *Journal-American*

Bystanders said that the dead man had been in good spirits all during the week.

St. Petersburg (Fla.) *Evening Independent*

A college president who can make buckwheat cakes turn flipflops on three girls simultaneously was reported today at Western College.

Cincinnati (Ohio) *Post*

Firemen must have served two sears in the department to be eligible for the engineer's exam.

Waco (Tex.) *Tribune*

Miss Rogers was winking for the third time when the life guard seized her and dragged her ashore.

Payson (Calif.) *Star*

Mr. and Mrs. George Willson were released from the Hazard hospital where they had been taken after being overcome by social gas in their home Saturday night.

Asbury Park (N.J.) *Press*

Their union was the result of eleven children.

St. Louis (Mo.) *Globe-Democrat*

Van Mert walked off with his room after remaining at Diekelmann's hotel several days and mailed it back at his own expense from Germany.

Johnson City (Tenn.) *Chronicle*

Returning home after having served several years as a missionary in the Congo, Mrs. Bedwell stated that the natives were often a bunch of howling sausages.

Fort Smith (Ark.) *News*

The mayor said that, though the Juneau police department has not been increased in size, crime has been going up rapidly.

Juneau (Alaska) *Daily Alaska Empire*

Thinking it was a waiter, opened it and in stormed Mrs. Calvert with an armful of private detectives.

Boston (Mass.) *Herald*

Dear Miss Dix:
I have been going steady for several months with my current boy friend. How long should I wait before telling him I am pregnant?

Buffalo (N.Y.) *Times*

The student may be reinstated only if absences are caused by long continued illness or death.

Granville (Ohio) *Denisonian*

Mr. Long and Bud Moore went deer hunting and shot a deer at Jonesboro. Also their guest, Alan Hancock, from Ashland, Maine.

Machias Valley (Me.) *News-Observer*

The American Legion band will play for the afternoon, and the athletic program will include races, swimming events and a series of mush-ball games, with a game for the championship of the district as the final. At 6 o'clock, picnic suppers will be served in Miller's grave.

Butler (Pa.) *Eagle*

Fire Captain Martin was hurt today when he fell ten feet through a skylight atop a private garage.
A strike of journeymen barbers was afire.

New York (N.Y.) *Times*

Lucille Ball doesn't know it to this minute, but she and Mrs. Walter Lang had on the same black sequin-top chiffon cocktail gown.

New York (N.Y.) *Journal-American*

The Earl of Antrim at Glenarm, England, has given birth to healthy twin calves twice in eleven months.

Walla Walla (Wash.) *Union*

Mr. Banks will be at Padgett's barbershop, starting Saturday, and states that he is again available for butchering livestock.

Kingman (Kan.) *Journal*

The fallen idol is portrayed by Bette Davis. She is rescued from the butter by Franchot Tone.

Charleston (S.C.) *Post*

Among the smallest screen stars are the following: Dorothy Janis, 4 feet 11 inches; May McAvoy, Betty Bronson and Bessie Love, all feet.

Birmingham (Ala.) *Age-Herald*

One unusual feature is a so-called bachelor's chamber with a fireplace and private bathroom. The maid's bedrooms and bath are conveniently located and are reached by a private stairway.

New Haven (Conn.) *Journal-Courier*

Bessie Schlacker, artist, today was completely recovered from an automobile accident in which she lost an arm and a leg. She amazed witnesses by walking to a hospital for treatment after the crash. The limps were artificial.

Worcester (Mass.) *Gazette*

The reunion was a great success. Especially liked was the 300-minute cocktail period immediately preceeding the business meeting.

New Orleans (La.) *Times-Picayune*

The main problem at Getchell, Pistell said, was to eliminate the large arsenic content for the remaining ore and to burn off the arsenic in such a way as not to pollute the air of nearby communities. This proved quite difficult in the early stages and was not entirely successful. "Unhappily," he said, "we killed off nearly all the dogs and cats and some nearby towns before the problem was solved."

Chicago (Ill.) *Daily News*

Ticket sale for "Sin Along with Mitch" at Boston Garden opens tomorrow.

Milton (Mass.) *Record-Transcript*

It was one of those rare vocal threats that one is fortunate to experience once in a life time.

Nashville (Tenn.) *Banner*

The United States Civil Defense has just published a book on fallout shelters. It will probably be found among the best cellars.

New York (N.Y.) *Times*

He estimated that the baby, born prematurely, was about seven months of age at the time of birth.

Clarksburg (W. Va.) *Exponent-Telegram*

This was Beckley's third trial. At each he admitted he shot his wife and stepdaughter, but said the women's attitude toward ham had goaded him to desperation.

San Francisco (Calif.) *Chronicle*

The Georgia Court of Appeals held: "Whenever the time comes that the sacredness of the jury box shall be invaded by any character of influenza—justice will flee from this court."

Lexington (Ky.) *Leader*

The holdup man was described as young, blond and crew-cut, wearing dark glasses and a four-inch revolver.

Los Angeles (Calif.) *Herald-Examiner*

Harry Wilcox of this city left today for a short business trip to Chicago. The Baptist Church of which he is a member will hold prayer services tonight.

Minneapolis (Minn.) *Star*

The deceased is survived by ten children, five of whom are living.

Hinton (W. Va.) *News*

Mayor Bass will spend the Fourth of July "just like any other day," he said yesterday. He will be in his office part of the day but will not attempt to transact any business.

Chattanooga (Tenn.) *Times*

The P.O. Dept. is never questioned. Every person who presents a letter for mailing is fully confident that it will be safely carried to its destruction.

Mountain Lake (Minn.) *Observer*

Cars and trains of a monorail system travel on a single overhead track instead of on the ground. They operate on the principle formerly used in many department stores to send cash swiftly between a salesperson and a central cashier in a small container.

Milwaukee (Wisc.) *Journal*

The New York debutante, whose runaway romance with the already married Porumbeanu flamed across two continents, returned Monday from Rome and is "in hiding" near New York, one of her closet friends revealed.

Harrisburg (Pa.) *Patriot*

The Engineering Women's Club will give an informal party at 8 p.m. on Friday. Mrs. William Cavett is chairman, assisted by Mrs. Robert Whats her name.

Ithaca (N.Y.) *Journal*

It's just disgusting to see women wear lipstick above their hip line.

Long Island (N.Y.) *Star-Journal*

The seaplane DO-X which took off this afternoon for Brazil made a forced descent sixty miles out in the ocean and a tub was dispatched to her assistance.

Passaic (N.J.) *Daily News*

The transport, carrying 55 passengers and a crew of 13, departed on a routine flight from Hickam Air Force Base near Honolulu to Moffet Field, a Navy Base. ttttt ttttt ttttt t hm hmhm Its No. 4 engine went dead when it was beyond the point of no return.

New Haven (Conn.) *Journal-Courier*

Treat the family to an extra chair, the kind every one wants to rest in. Freeman Electric.

Clay Center (Kan.) *Dispatch*

The Farm and Fireside Unit had its Christmas party at the home of Mrs. Frank Dumler. There were 20 members present; 11 were lucky to have their husbands as guests; the rest just enjoyed themselves.

Colby (Kan.) *Free Press-Tribune*

Miss Margaret Landers is driving a new car, also Freeman Nickerson.

Hyannis (Mass.) *Barnstable Patriot*

The Rotary chairman replied in a few appropriated remarks.

Fort Smith (Ark.) *Times Record*

Television Station WHP was off a matter of minutes, but the relief was short-lived.

Harrisburg (Pa.) *News*

The daughter of a well-to-do square married Queen Elizabeth's first cousin.

St. Petersburg (Fla.) *Independent*

In a way, it is all very confusing. If Sophie Tucker celebrated her 40th year in show business in 1947 and her 59th year in show business in 1953, why is and in reply asked, rather sensibly, why is it that 1964?

New York (N.Y.) *Post*

Mr. and Mrs. O. P. Elder entertained 25 little gusts at their home yesterday in honor of the eighth birthday of their son.

Greensburg (Pa.) *Morning Review*

Photographer Gene Webb who with his son Charles and Dr. Black went to Gatlinburg last week, got a good photograph of the icebound falls on the Roaring Creek road as they made a sheer plunge of seventy-five feet.

Nashville (Tenn.) *Banner*

He comes from a good family—appears refined, although intelligent.

Chicago (Ill.) *News*

Phyllis Brannon arrived in San Francisco after a six-weeks sea voyage from Antwerp. Her plans are to secure a bungalow and half a Chinaman, and to remain in California until it stops being winter along the Atlantic seaboard.

Boston (Mass.) *Globe*

The Sagona's doctors and nurses were scheduled to land last night, but messages indicated that the men probably would be married aboard the ship, receive first aid treatment, and then be taken to St. John's.

New York (N.Y.) *World-Telegram*

The noodle soup, the vegetables and sour cream, the stuffed cabbage and chopped liver—Mrs. Brown's own—have been the fare of many of the theatre stars who have come to Pittsburgh.

Pittsburgh (Pa.) *Press*

In addition, he is a sea-fighter of great courage, to which half-a-dozen World War meals attest.

Palo Alto (Calif.) *Daily Times*

Lieut. General Robert M. Morrison will address us on Air Defense in Europe—a subject about which a few people know more.

Los Angeles (Calif.) *Times*

Capital punishment applied to the wrong type of child—the nervous, sensitive type—may do irreparable harm.

Newcastle (England) *Journal*

Sam Fetterman has taken up farming in Arkansas, despite his intentions to reform his former habits.

Chattanooga (Tenn.) *Times*

Trees were uprooted in the residential section. Scores of persons were injured slightly by glass and lambs falling from trees.

Worcester (Mass.) *Evening Gazette*

Vada Pinson did not suffer serious injury when beaned in the first game after losing a curse in the white-shirted crowd background in the seventh inning of the opener.

Pittsburgh (Pa.) *Press*

A string of vehicles loaded with apples a quarter of a mile long at a cider-mill is a common sight.

Fort Wayne (Ind.) *News*

"The carnage on our highways can be reduced, but only if you give us the fools to perform the job," said Gov. Hatfield.

Oregon City (Ore.) *Enterprise-Courier*

A beautiful widow often will make up for ugly and cumbersome furniture.

White Plains (N.Y.) *Reporter Dispatch*

TWA's tourist excursion fare allowing 15 dull days abroad makes it possible to fly from New York to London and back for as little as $425.

New York (N.Y.) *Times*

Queen Elizabeth emerged in her new haid style for the first time.

St. Louis (Mo.) *Post-Dispatch*

For the first time in the history of the Women's Club, a past president's pin was presented to the retiring president. Nine new members were welcomed and presented red noses during the affair.

Bayside (N.Y.) *Times*

As they moved off, Peggy put her arm through Stanley's. He could feel her arm in his toes.

St. Louis (Mo.) *Post-Dispatch*

Jim Vlardy came home from Wyoming Tuesday evening on the train, where he had been all summer.

Eagle Valley (Colo.) *Enterprise*

The Post Office department has announced that while there will be no regular mail delivery Thanksgiving Day, a skeleton will maintain service for special delivery and perishable material.

Parkersburg (W. Va.) *News*

The income tax table is for simple persons and married couples filing joint returns.

Buffalo (N.Y.) *Evening News*

Mother can disassemble the boys at the end of play time and pack the little containers away neatly.

Newport News (Va.) *Times-Herald*

The show will be concluded with a massed aerial "attack" on the airport by members of the Naval Air Reserve. From a rendezvous at 10,000 feet the "weekend warriors" will pee off in steep dives and will roar across the field in mock straffing runs.

Niagara Falls (N.Y.) *Gazette*

The ladies of the Helping Hand Society enjoyed a swap social on Friday evening. Everybody brought something they didn't need. Many of the ladies were accompanied by their husbands.

Middlesex (Mass.) *News*

The world's champion eater of sweet corn is Edward Kottwitz, of Ortonville, who ate 37 years at one sitting. Those who witnessed him set the "record" say that he ate without napkin and did not once get his ears or hair mussy.

Ortonville (Minn.) *Independent*

The worst story in recent Detroit history swept over the heart of the city late today, killing two persons, unroofing several buildings, uprooting trees, shattering windows and damaging hundreds of automobiles.

Indianapolis (Ind.) *Times*

Returning to the Mainland, members have a choice of flying or sailing to San Francisco on the Matson Line's luxurious SS *Lurline*.

San Francisco (Calif.) *Chronicle*

Other guests at the banquet included Clinton's football coach, press representatives and Mr. and Mrs. Damifinow.

Clinton (Iowa) *Herald*

But the testimony of a fourth corner to the love triangle started their tongues clicking again.

St. Louis (Mo.) *Globe-Democrat*

Her mouth twisted downward and suddenly her composure was gone and she was sobbing and screaming in muted agony.

New York (N.Y.) *Journal-American*

79

A three-day growth of beard covers many an honest heart.

Gloucester (Mass.) *Times*

The two women will celebrate their birthdays Friday with family gatherings at their respective homes and will probably get together with their husbands at least once during the day.

De Pere (Wisc.) *Journal-Democrat*

Dispatches from Tsinan said Japanese residents were preparing to evaporate and go to Tsingtao.

Atlanta (Ga.) *Journal*

The House passed a bill designed to protect television and radio stations from demands for squal time on news programs by candidates for office.

Pittsburgh (Pa.) *Post-Gazette*

Fred V. Vance, deputy grand exhausted ruler of the Elks, will visit Johnson City on Thursday.

Johnson City (Tenn.) *Press-Chronicle*

The officer said he found three empty glasses, a half-gallon demijohn and three empty flasks near the body. Death is believed to have been due to natural causes.

San Francisco (Calif.) *Chronicle*

During the absence of our pastor we enjoyed the rare privilege of hearing a good sermon, when Mr. J. A. Watts supplied our pulpit. We hope he will come again.

Omaha (Nebr.) *Church Bulletin*

The Texas bankers were justified in offering a reward for the killing of dead bank robbers.

Pueblo (Colo.) *Chieftain*

The operator of the other car, charged with drunken driving, crashed into Miss Miller's rear end which was sticking out into the road.

Osage (Iowa) *Press News*

Outwardly calm, and with no apparent emotion, Marian Myers, ex-university co-ed, heard Circuit Judge Beck sentence her to thirty days in the State penitentiary yesterday for her attempt to rob a bank here February 5. She had firsts, 43½¢; butterfat, steady; medium, eggs, 1¢ lower, 17¢.

Longview (Wash.) *News*

He was born in early life in Franklin county.

Columbia (S.C.) *State*

On the other hand, Miss Wethered played steadolly bm bm bm bm

New York (N.Y.) *Morning Telegraph*

Read our new booklet, "How To Increase Your Word Power, Think Better, Spell Perrectly."

San Antonio (Tex.) *Express*

The Reading Company may be forced to reduce its personnel. Deceased revenues, the officials declared, can be blamed when the necessity arises.

Philadelphia (Pa.) *Evening Bulletin*

H. H. Hill has been taking port in a program of alcohol education sponsored by the Manitoba Temperance Alliance.

Winnipeg (Canada) *Free Press*

Howard Wilson suffered a broken leg Saturday night while changing a tire on the pavement.

Cresco (Iowa) *News*

In discussing plans for the new 1 story skyscraper being erected on Broadway, Sanderson, the architect, stated that the first floor would be used for parking.

New York (N.Y.) *Times*

Consequently Betty has been flipping around on the trapeze ever since she got the part. Dorothy Lamour has been swinging by her teets to perfect her role as the "Iron Jaw" girl.

Santa Ana (Calif.) *Register*

While attending services at Highland Friends' church Saturday, four heifers owned by Homer Phillips escaped from the pasture and were killed by a freight train.

Salem (Ind.) *Democrat*

After 64 years, the New York University School of Commerce is getting a new name. In September it will become the New York University School of Commerce.

New York (N.Y.) *University Alumni News*

She wore a tailored suit and her corsage was an orchard.

Luling (Tex.) *Newsboy*

Fire of undetermined origin swept through the new Dinuba High School today and destroyed the $150,000 structure, and went back to work.

San Francisco (Calif.) *Examiner*

Father Time was rebuffed here in the annual Father-Son race when Dr. O. R. Austin, veteran physician, met the challenge of youth and defeated his 244-year-old son, Harold, in the 50-yard sprint race.

Meridian (Miss.) *Star*

In some States the shooting of young ducks is also forbidden, and there the hunter must first count the points of his quarry's antlers.

Appleton (Wisc.) *Post-Crescent*

Apart from the duty of preserving the peace and protecting crime, the Police Department has many other tasks.

New York (N.Y.) *Times*

Mrs. Albert Swanson and Mrs. Ole Koland attended the sale of a relative Saturday.

Sandstone (Minn.) *Pine County Courier*

Mr. and Mrs. Clayton Davis have returned home after a week-end trip to their lake on a cabin in Northwest Arkansas.

Van Buren (Ark.) *Press Argus*

An unusual touch was added to the wedding scene, when four young Omaha debts appeared as bridesmaids.

Omaha (Nebr.) *World-Herald*

Mrs. Felix Favier of 7 Sunshine Court is at the Massachusetts Women's Hospital in Boston for a chuck-up.

Newport (R.I.) *News*

The child was hurried to Bukharest for anti-rabies treatment and an official bulletin says his condition is not dangerous. The dog was immediately killed. His father is the former Crown Prince Carol.

Cleveland (Ohio) *Plain Dealer*

Col. Martin L. Crimmins, U.S.A., retired, was bitten by a water mocassin just before he was to have delivered an address on poisonous snakes.

Buffalo (N.Y.) *News*

The Police Department announced today that girls wearing bikinis will be put in the hands of low enforcement officers.

Miami Beach (Fla.) *Daily Sun*

Good grammer and accent are offensive to nobody.

Tahlequah (Okla.) *North-eastern*

Three hundred thousand Freshmen will enter American institutions of higher yearning next fall.

Princeton (N.J.) *Seminary Bulletin*

A helicopter was used to save 13 trapped and starving cattle from snowpacked mountainous terrain 10,000 feet below sea level.

St. Joseph (Mo.) *News-Press*

Last week the NYRA hired a politician who has had no background in racing, and is now on the NYRA pad for a yearly salary in five fingers.

New York (N.Y.) *Daily Mirror*

For this new venture Mike Wallace has assembled a staff of experienced reporters and a full-time crow to do film coverage.

New York (N.Y.) *Herald Tribune*

The bride wore an aquamarine floor-length gown with fuchsia trimming and carried an old-fashioned.

Greenfield (Mass.) *Recorder-Gazette*

The party was held for all the centenarians of the town. Included among the guests were Mr. and Mrs. Hiram Crawford, Alex Metcalfe and Mrs. Lorene Jackson. Also present was Irving Phillips, the town coroner and undertaker.

Fort Smith (Ark.) *Times Record*

Many of these old houses have been torn down to make way for parking lots and factories, he said. Many mothers, he said, have fallen into disrepair for lack of interest and should be restored and utilized by individuals and societies, conscious of their traditional beauty and historical significance.

Quincy (Mass.) *Patriot Ledger*

Thelma Sagely, seventy-seven, was struck by an automobile when she roller-skated into the street in front of her home.

Cincinnati (Ohio) *Enquirer*

The last round of parties for and in the Pendennis Castle is now in full swig.

Cape Town (South Africa) *Cape Times*

If these export credits can be arranged, and Carl Williams of the Board said that satisfactory progress was being made, the sales would be on a cash basis, with the banks doing the purchasers.

Detroit (Mich.) *Free Press*

Several phone calls have informed us that the photo we used last Wednesday of Fred Martin was actually that of his brother, Phillip. However, it should have been that of Homer McWilliams. May we ask all of our subscribers to just ignore the whole thing?

Van Buren (Ark.) *Press Argus*

A bay boy was born today at the Colton hospital to Mr. and Mrs. Marvin Schus.

Colton (Calif.) *Courier*

The soprano was asked to sing. She sank "Just a Song at Twilight."

Birmingham (Ala.) *Post Herald*

Harry Lawson, U.S.N., is spending a fifteen-day furlough at his home. He recently recovered from burns

86

and injuries received when a gun backfired, after being in a naval hospital several weeks.

Winsted (Conn.) *Evening Citizen*

For the first time in several months, County Judge Frank G. Mirick late Friday married Mrs. Manilla Roberts and Virgil A. Bailey, both of Pueblo.

Pueblo (Colo.) *Star-Journal*

Receiving guests were the honoree, her mother, Mrs. Williams in a silver chafing dish.

Birmingham (Ala.) *Post Herald*
Denton (Tex.) *Record-Chronicle*

A revised edition of the Pocono Manor Inn's map of its 3,000-acre grounds is not available to guests to help them locate the various facilities and activities.

New York (N.Y.) *Journal-American*

I am going to enforce trespassing and hunting on the farms posted in my name so it's up to you from now on.

La Grande (Ore.) *Observer*

Two men were decapitated and then burned to death.

Washington (D.C.) *Evening Star*

Mr. and Mrs. W. Edwin Gledhill and Mrs. J. K. Lewis are in Los Angeles attending the Pacific Southwest tennis tournament in which their son, Keith, is participating.

Los Angeles (Calif.) *Times*

Strangers and friends alike stop for the second look at the two-headed freckle-faced boy when he works out at the Orlando Tennis Club.

Brownsville (Tex.) *Herald*

Stealing the sow at the Jefferson Gallery, a woman in mink stole and shorts looking over the Picasso exhibit.

San Diego (Calif.) *Evening Tribune*

Touching a high tension wire as he was climbing on the framework of an abandoned bride over Mill Creek, James Leas, 15 years old, had a double escape from death.

Cincinnati (Ohio) *Post & Times-Star*

Two groups were examined. One was comprised of 40 lawmakers; the other, 40 persons who had committed no crimes.

Rochester (N.Y.) *Democrat & Chronicle*

Falling on the icy pavement, he broke three things; his left arm, a bottle of whiskey, and the third commandment.

Fort Smith (Ark.) *News*

Judge Jones ordered the room cleared of all persons except interested parties, 999 attorneys, court officials and a reporter.

El Dorado (Ark.) *News*

Mayor Harry B. Heaton has found a new use for confiscated liquor. When poured on the walls and interior of the city jailer, it proves successful as an exterminator of cockroaches and bedbugs. The Mayor says the bugs drink the stuff, some dying outright and others becoming so intoxicated they fall, breaking their necks.

Columbus (Ohio) *Dispatch*

Rev. E. M. Coe of Cleveland, with 27 recent convicts, will come to Livingston Wednesday evening for the purpose of administering the rites of baptism.

Houston (Tex.) *Post*

Eighteen miners who were burned alive in a cavern at the Houssu colliery near Mons were rescued during the night, unharmed.

Louisville (Ky.) *Times*

He was united in marriage to Miss Morton, June 20. The deceased bore his affliction with patience and courage that was beautiful.

Joliet (Ill.) *Herald-News*

Topeka's Jeffersonian Club will hold its annual Washington Day tea on Lincoln's Birthday.

Topeka (Kan.) *State Journal*

In most associations half the committee does all the work, whilst the other half does nothing. I am pleased to put on record that in this society it is just the reverse.

Liverpool (England) *Echo*

L.B.J.'s charming daughter, Luci Baines, will be seen on the TV show in two parts.

Chicago (Ill.) *Daily Tribune*

The princess is a daughter of the illustrious House of Tokugawa, which for two and one-half centuries supplied the shotguns that actually ruled the empire.

Lafayette (La.) *Advertiser*

He was met at the railroad station by representatives of the British crown, foreign office dignitaries, army and navy officers. Actually, and not figuratively, a red plush carpet was rolled down to make his entrance diplomatically hotsytotsy, hoisted aboard ship by slings passed under their bodies.

Livermore (Me.) *Advertiser*

On her 80th birthday, Mrs. W. H. Erwin received the present she wanted most, a portable typewriter. She'd just recently learned to tope.

San Diego (Calif.) *Tribune*

A dull red fish mounts from beneath the black collar of her dress. She moves uneasily in her chair.

Yonkers (N.Y.) *Herald Statesman*

It's always fun to be with a person who listens with courteous attention and obvious interest when you are doing toe talking.

Redlands (Calif.) *Daily Facts*

Throwing the cigarette away, he seated himself upon her entering.

Dallas (Tex.) *Times-Herald*

From his left ear to the corner of his mouth ran a long scar, the result of a duet many years before.

Harrisburg (Pa.) *News*

"Angel" for the ball, attended by 400 benefit-goers, was Fred B. Snite, who asked to remain anonymous.

Chicago (Ill.) *Tribune*

This is the fifth of a series of articles written by a woman who recently crossed, alone, on two of the White Star ships.

Daytona Beach (Fla.) *Journal*

Winds whistled through the Central Plains, the upper part of the Southern Plains, around the Great Ladies and in the Rockies.

Augusta (Ga.) *Herald*

At the November PTA bake sale and card party, a cake was sold to someone in an oblong aluminum cake pan about two inches high, with grooves for a cover.

Kendall County (Ill.) *News*

The meeting will be held at 2 p.m. in the Society's room on the second floor of the Flemington Library Building. Any who are not members and are not interested are invited to attend.

Flemington (N.J.) *Democrat*

Arrangements are complete for the lecture by Count Felix Von Luckner, one of Germany's greatest aviators during the World War, when he shot down probably more Allied aircraft than any other German sea captain.

Superior (Wisc.) *Telegram*

Clyde Pierson, Middletown, brought seven of the boys of his Sunday school class out to Phillips' sugar camp last Friday night and camped out. They slept on straw in the sugarhouse and cooked their vitals on the furnace. This was a great time for those boys.

Eaton (Ohio) *Register-Herald*

The President has a recommendation that $5,000,000 be spent on his desk.

Oil City (Pa.) *Derrick*

The union and the railroad agreed that adequate and ample babooses would be supplied.

Syracuse (N.Y.) *Herald-Journal*

A southeast girl with a wind velocity of fifty miles an hour was reported to be sweeping Bay St. Louis.

New York (N.Y.) *Mirror*

Burdette had gone to the mouse to attempt a reconciliation. She refused to listen to his pleas.

Wilmington (Del.) *Every Evening*

Miss Sibyl Baker will conduct a course in how to grow old at the YWCA.

Washington (D.C.) *Evening Star*

The Federal Aviation Agency's rules for takeoffs and landings of jet-powered transports include this sentence: "The takeoff distance shall not be greater than the length of the runway."

(New York, N.Y.) United Press International

Architect Marcel Breuer characteristically designed such interiors in the home of fabric printer George Neumann and his designing wife Vera (shown in black and white in our June 1956 issue.)

New York (N.Y.) *Interiors*

The Murphy Oil Corp. will market a new method of dispensing gasoline which is designed to match a grade of gas with a specific horsepower of car engine. At Murphy stations, motorists will be given a choice of five different gasoline blends to match with the horsepower rating, said John J. McClure, marketing vice-president.

The motorists will also be dispensed from one pump.

New Orleans (La.) *States-Item*

The cutworm, that menace to tomato growers and also to many other species of vegetables, is again making its appearance.

Brockton (N.Y.) *Beacon*

"Of course I'm a fan. I'm from Pittsburgh and I go whenever they play the Yankees. One day Yogi Berra hit a home run and I caught it. I was sitting in my lucky seat, right behind the dugout."

New York (N.Y.) *World-Telegram & Sun*

Internal Revenue officials said they may be able to extend a little help to confuse taxpayers struggling with their income tax forms after all.

Tallahassee (Fla.) *Capital Post*

The new Miss America will be drowned later before a nationwide television audience.

Atlantic City (N.J.) *Press*

The boys decided that would be the most enjoyable way of winning Jean's hand and heat.

Xenia (Ohio) *Gazette*

Bangert also finds time to serve as president of the Peoples Athletic League, an organization which raises funds to send underprivileged boys to Summer girls.

New York (N.Y.) *Daily Mirror*

What is needed now worse than anything else is a warm dry rain.

New York (N.Y.) *Daily News Record*

On arrival in Portland the train will be met by a delegation of Portland Rotarians and taken on an auto tour of the city.

Boston (Mass.) *Herald*

She was graduated from Huntington High School and has been employed as a secretary in New York City. Her husband is a buyer for a Philadelphia Dept. Store and deserved four years in the U. S. Air Force.

New York (N.Y.) *Long Island Press*

Mrs. C. J. Keppel entertained twenty of the wives of the Cranbrook faculty at a stag bridge and supper.

Detroit (Mich.) *Free Press*

I used to hide in corners at parties and blush when spoken to but now a pin drop is audible as I rise,

94

poised, perfect and primed, to toast my hose at a banquet.

Erie (Pa.) *News*

A covered-dish supper will be served by the Truth Seekers Bible Class on Wednesday evening at 6:30. Husbands of members are also invited. Don't forget to bring the "cats!"

Bethlehem (Pa.) *Globe-Times*

A moment later he was the soul of paternal tenderness as he passed out a suggestion to the 100 ballet girls, the forty-eight Roxyettes, and the 100 choristers. "I want all you kids to keep grinning, no matter what happens." The kids grinned, showing 350 rows of teeth. It was all very regimental.

New York (N.Y.) *Herald Tribune*

The list also included Mrs. Rene Bouche, Mr. and Mrs. William Colleran, Mr. and Mrs. Martin Gabel, Alan Jay Lerner and Oliver Messel, Lord Snowden's uncle. The Livingston Biddles had declined, and Mr. Blass sent his regrets. Truman Capote, on the other hand, did not answer his invitation.

Charlotte (N.C.) *Observer*

A table brought to America on the Mayflower and a bulkhead odor from the U.S.S. Mine were among 2,337 gifts the Chicago Historical Society received last year.

Chicago (Ill.) *Daily News*

With 23½ pints, the two ladies were high players in four tables of duplicate bridge.

Martinsburg (W. Va.) *Journal*

Four thousand square miles of untouched virgin were reported in Labrador.

Augusta (Me.) *Kennebec Journal*

In India the Nizam has diamonds by the bushel, it is said, and incalculable quantities of gold and germs.

Philadelphia (Pa.) *Evening Bulletin*

Although it was late at night, she walked in upon his invitation.

Denver (Colo.) *Rocky Mountain News*

Miss Beulah Williams, a Batesville belle of twenty summers, is visiting her twin brother, age thirty-two.

Batesville (Ark.) *Guard*

His Imperial Majesty yesterday received Premier Mansur in audience. During the three-hour long audience, Mr. Mansur delivered a state-of-the-nation report to the Shah. Later, Mr. Mansur returned home and attended to state affairs while in bed.

Tehran (Iran) *Kayhan*

Another of those splendid Danish programs will be broadcasted over WTMJ tonight from 12:30 to 3 in the yawning.

Milwaukee (Wisc.) *Journal*

The Knights of Columbus will unveil a new mural of Columbus landing in the clubrooms at Grace and Eighth Streets.

Richmond (Va.) *News Leader*

Guest of honor for what may yet prove to be a monotonous occasion will be Garland C. Routt.

Dublin (Ireland) *Irish Independent*

Simmons got the longest drive of the day when he hit one to right field and caught the ball 5 feet from the bleacher fence.

Mount Prospect (Ill.) *Independent*

One of the best investments a farmer can make at this season of the year is money spent in paint. As a rule, the farmer can put the paint on himself and in so doing brighten up the home.

Aberdeen (Wash.) *World*

Charles Watson, completely for his own amazement, invented a new type of automobile brake.

San Francisco (Calif.) *Chronicle*

Around 4 p.m., employees of a furniture concern arrived at the apartment with a cough which had been upholstered.

Cleveland (Ohio) *Plain Dealer*

There, a young Indian and his companion found Mr. Gibson, who broke his ankle when his plane crashed yesterday on the floor next to an electric heater.

Albany (N.Y.) *Times-Union*

Purpose of the survey is to determine whether the mark-ups prescribed by OPS fool regulations are realistic.

Mitchell (S.D.) Daily Republic

Martin Behrman, 61, Mayor of New Orleans for his fifth term, died today, after an extended illness. Behrman was born here when he was one year old.

Hartford (Conn.) Times

Five firemen were hurt and eleven injured.

Saugerties (N.Y.) Post

The Rev. Hamilton spoke briefly much to the delight of the audience.

Warren (Ohio) Church Bulletin

The driver of the coupe jumped from the car and ran, they said, after the accident. The couple struck another car before striking the man. Officers who investigated found seven cases of contraband corn whiskey in the driver of the car.

Columbia (S.C.) Record

Elizabeth Hopkins, 26, Tacoma, Wash., arrested yesterday as she was hitch-hiking nude, was sentenced by Daly City Police Judge William Sweeney to 30 days in jail—for having no visible means of support.

Charleston (S.C.) News and Courier

The percentage of correctly prepared tax returns increased sharply but numerous simple misrakes continue to show up.

Pembina (N.D.) New Era

Walker, a worker on one of Corson County's newly started bridge projects, was reported here Tuesday to have received two broken legs and several fractured legs when an embankment on a bridge near McLaughlin caved in.

Aberdeen (S.D.) *American-News*

Carelessness on the part of two visitors at the Eastport Fire Company's carnival Saturday night resulted in injury to both. Robert Bentley, twenty-three, is in the Emergency Hospital rather seriously injured as a result of a fall. A small Negro boy was injured when he fell from a revolving apparatus. The carnival is proving a worthwhile attraction.

Annapolis (Md.) *Evening Capital*

Asked if his organization (the Nassau County Patrolmen's Benevolent Association), which has 2,200 members, is in conflict with the statute, Patrolman Lecci said: "This is still a free country. As president of the P.B.A., I have every right in the world to tell members how to vote."

New York (N.Y.) *Times*

Microphone trouble beset Jayne Mansfield but her sequined chest and skillfully designed bras got a lot of attention anyway.

Los Angeles (Calif.) *Mirror*

The Philadelphia 76ers will go into Boston Garden Thursday night needing two victories in one game against the Boston Celtics to cinch the Eastern Division title of the National Basketball Association.

Fort Smith (Ark.) *Southwest American*

99

"But," Dr. Leeson says, "we're happy to get cadavers at any price and we'll settle for a change in legislation that will help to maintain an adequate supply."

New York (N.Y.) *Medical Tribune*

The Rev. Bunts preached a very earnest and impressive discourse based on the conversation of Lydia under the teaching of St. Paul and then extended a cordial invitation to the unshaved to come forward.

West Union (Ohio) *People's Defender*

A little dear is running around at night in the vicinity of Seneca Junction.

Olean (N.Y.) *Times Herald*

Game Warden W. E. Alberts has announced that only two pleasant hunting days will be permitted in succession with the remainder distributed.

Oskaloosa (Iowa) *Herald*

Mary looked smart in a pale pink frock as she catted about her husband and their proposed trip to California.

El Paso (Tex.) *Herald-Post*

Martin C. Rusch has gone to Hot Springs, Ark., for his annual bath.

Minocqua (Wisc.) *Lakeland Times*

Youth Temperance Council members this afternoon will visit Endless Taverns.

Newport News (Va.) *Daily Press*

Mr. and Mrs. Sidney Bomberg entertained Mr. and Mrs. Thomas Flynn and their eight-year-old son at dinner Friday night. A good time was had by all, except Sidney, Jr., who stated that he did not have a good time.

Tarpon Springs (Fla.) *Leader*

The valley offers romance, history, sport, scenery of unsurpassed beauty, a mecca for art lovers and dames that are marvels of modern engineering.

Keene (N.H.) *Sentinel*

We have been fortunate, indeed, to have Mr. Kalinke visit us and when he leaves we will be more than thankful.

Clarkston (Mich.) *News*

The names and addresses of the team Managers have been sent to the company. They promised to gum things up from there.

Pittston (Pa.) *Dispatch*

Perkins was chief sock-holder in a hotel and bank.

San Antonio (Tex.) *Express*

The combined circulation of the Courier and The Saturday Evening Post now has reached 4,600,500.

Van Buren (Ark.) *Courier*

Do not say, "We have proof of this having happened." It is much better to say, "We have proof that this has hoppened."

Ludington (Mich.) *Daily News*

After his crackup in 1931, Walt obeyed his doctor's orders to acquire outside interests. As a result, he wound up with a string of polo ponies and a daughter named Diane.

Philadelphia (Pa.) *Inquirer*

To find the nearest club, look up Alcoholics Anonymous. To find the nearest club, look up Alcoholics in the phone book. There are over 4500 such groups, and they don't ask how rich or and they don't ask how rich or poor you are, or anything else except, "Can we help youz?"

Worcester (Mass.) *Evening Gazette*

Bobby Jones, one of the world's best-loved poets, will be honored Sunday with a program of Scotch, song, and poetry.

Columbus (Ohio) *Sunday Dispatch*

We are happy to report that Mrs. James C. Callahan has not been so well the past two weeks and is again confined to her bed.

Los Angeles (Calif.) *Times*

It is known that four Somerville school-teachers have married since July 10, and at last two in Cambridge.

Boston (Mass.) *Sunday Globe*

Among the gifts of the bridegroom to the bride was a beautiful pressing down.

Buffalo (N.Y.) *Times*

He struck the car in which she was riding broadside.

Dallas (Tex.) *Oak Cliff Tribune*

A suburban real estate boom appears inevitable. 15 to 20 million dollars will purchase nearly 100 acres of beautiful rolling land about 2 miles west of Minneapolis, on new highway. Bus, schools and other conveniences. There is risk in this investment, but a tremendous profit is sure.

Minneapolis (Minn.) *Tribune*

The authority's plans presently call for the construction of a trunk pipe with an 84-inch diameter which will carry Middlesex County down the Raritan River and empty it out into the bay 4,500 feet from the Keansburg shore.

Long Branch (N.J.) *Daily Record*

Not only old members will die; young ones will too, from sickness, on-the-job accidents, automobile smash-ups and other causes. But when a beneficiary member of the B&CW sees Death looming up, that long split second as a car crashes with a sickening crunch of crushed metal and flying glass, it's too late for him to cry as his life is snuffed out:

"I wish I had changed my beneficiary."

St. Louis (Mo.) *Post-Dispatch*

We invite everyone to visit the new theater and feel that you will be more than delighted with the arrangement, convenience and modern way in which it is built and equipped. Nothing has been spared to mar the comfort of the patrons.

Bluefield (W. Va.) *Telegraph*

The program is continued with a horse show and the latter is composed entirely of members of the faculty.

Middletown (Conn.) *Press*

Muncie school children will wreck their young brains again in an attempt to win the slogan contest.

Muncie (Ind.) *Evening Press*

She was a wholesome young woman who regretted that their income was too small for them to have children.

Van Buren (Ark.) *Press Argus*

Two days later his doctor allowed him to pick up his bed and talk.

New York (N.Y.) *News-Magazine*

A Thanksgiving dinner was served at the home of Mr. and Mrs. Penton, after the wedding of their daughter.

Poughkeepsie (N.Y.) *Journal*

For the premiere, Dance No. 1 by Brahms; "La Gitana," by Kreisler, and "Then I'll Be Tired of Kreisler," and "Then I'll Be Tired of You," by Schwartz.

Boston (Mass.) *Traveler*

Skelly, who was accompanied by his wife, had other troubles, too.

Atlantic City (N.J.) *Press*

During the winter season last year, Mr. and Mrs. Adam Imboden of Bradenton, Fla., entertained 65 visitors from the North.

The Imbodens recently sold their large beautiful ranch-style home and purchased a smaller dwelling.

Schuylkill Haven (Pa.) *Call*

The store will open for business January 13. You will have no difficulty finding your way about, as there will be uninformed attendants on every floor.

Seabeck (Wash.) *News-Advertiser*

After quickly taking a second drink, Jorgenson walked into the office of the president and demanded more celery in his pay envelope each week.

Little Rock (Ark.) *Democrat*

Loving models are used by members of the O. A. C. Art Club at their Tuesday night meetings.

Portland (Ore.) *Reporter*

Simon & Schuster have published *My Little Golden Dictionary* for children. Dr. Mary Reed and Edith Osswald ate the authors and Richard Scarry the illustrator.

Greensboro (N.C.) *Daily News*

The main street will be well decorated by the businessmen and the residents should be lighted up to match.

Gretna (Nebr.) *Breeze*

The rifle club of the N. and W. Railway Y.M.C.A., Portsmouth, Ohio, will shoot ten men in a fifty-yard muzzle-loading match.

New York (N.Y.) *American Rifleman*

John Weinberger, who was run down at the same time, died of his injuries. Last night his temperature declined somewhat.

Wilkes-Barre (Pa.) *Times-Leader*

In a finish you'd have to see to believe, Springfield Griffin won the 25th high school basketball championship of Illinois today by defeating Niles West with three runs in the last half of the seventh inning, 6 to 5.

Chicago (Ill.) *Tribune*

What is more beautiful for the blonde to wear for formal dances than white tulle? My answer—and I'm sure you'll agree with me—is "Nothing."

Worcester (Mass.) *Evening Gazette*

Local police are puzzled over the finding of a car parked outside the Methodist Church containing a full case of Scotch whiskey. So far they have found no trace of the owner, but Captain Casey is diligently working on the case.

Muscatine (Iowa) *Journal*

Mr. and Mrs. Morrison left Wednesday for Rochester, where Mrs. Morrison expects to have a garter removed by the Mayo brothers.

Fairmont (Minn.) *Sentinel*

A feature of the handiwork exhibit was an infant knitted by Mrs. Joseph Fenton.

New Bedford (Mass.) *Standard-Times*

The program will include a series of short skirts, designed to appeal to all ages.

Oneonta (N.Y.) *Star*

Wearing black hunting cap, brown coat, tan jodh-purs and black boots, Mrs. Kennedy took a boy mare named Princess over four jumps.

New York (N.Y.) *Journal-American*

One can peek in most any evening on this home-loving young actress and find her cuddled up in an easy chair with a good boob before a crackling log fire.

Hollywood (Calif.) *Citizen-News*

Mrs. Crockett filed the bill which extended daylight saving time in Massachusetts through October. Her argument was it would prolong the twilight hours when most automobile accidents occur.

Providence (R.I.) *Journal*

A twenty-two-year-old woman saved three bothers from drowning yesterday.

Indianapolis (Ind.) *Star*

Construction operations are scheduled to start Mon-day, the fireproof, double-sided owner announced.

Norfolk (Nebr.) *Daily News*

Unmarried, John E. Hollingsworth was born Sep-tember 9th, 1907.

Fargo (N.D.) *Forum-News*

President Johnson called in Cabinet officers and heads of Government agencies today to report on his cost-cutting drive in Government and to urge they continuetheireconomyefforts.

Washington (D.C.) *Daily News*

The persecution is being handled by the district attorney.

Albany (N.Y.) *Knickerbocker News*

Members of the posse took refuse behind a farmhouse and kept up a running fire, but the bandits dashed to their automobile and sped away.

Philadelphia (Pa.) *Evening Public Ledger*

Young Brownley was burned some about his head. Not much damage was done.

De Kalb (Ill.) *Chronicle*

Among the passengers is William Todd, who lies in Tahiti.

Birmingham (Ala.) *News*

For the less formal interior, straight-hanging, unlined draw curtains are helpful in creating an atmosphere of intimate hostility.

Portland (Ore.) *Journal*

The instant the driver is ready to shift he simply raises his foot to the accelerator pedal and he is ready to start away in the next year.

Pittsburgh (Pa.) *Press*

108

Fast growth is more important to animals than to other flowers because they have so little time to reach maternity.

Covington (Va.) *Virginian*

The resignation of the manager is to become effective on or before November 1, or earlier if possible.

Denison (Iowa) *Bulletin*

Clinton observed Veterans' Day with a special ceremony Saturday. The American Legion Post and other pathetic organizations conducted services on the east side of the courthouse square.

Clinton (Ill.) *Journal*

Miriam Hopkins stars as Mrs. Kry, a recluse whose life revolves around the small black box into which her bridegroom disappeared on their wedding day in 1929.

Seattle (Wash.) *Daily Times*

Baron Yusaburo, 800-year-old president of the Privy Council, resigned today because of advancing age.

San Antonio (Tex.) *Light*

Early Romans exchanged hands as a sign of friendship.

New York (N.Y.) *Herald Tribune*

The lion of Lucerne is a memorial to the Swiss Guards who died defending Louis XVI from a job during the French revolution.

Raleigh (N.C.) *News and Observer*

But two children, a boy and a girl, will remember until they sit with grandmothers about their knees.

Los Angeles (Calif.) *Times*

A very fine time was reported, a few regretted being able to be present.

Moravia (N.Y.) *Republican Register*

In addition to the turkey, the State's charges will feast upon 18,000 pounds of sweet potatoes, 9,000 pounds of bananas, 1,500 pounds of almonds, 5,000 pounds of candy, and neckties, sweaters, stockings and other gifts.

San Francisco (Calif.) *Chronicle*

His father commanded a fleet of ships that piled the North Pacific from San Francisco.

Los Angeles (Calif.) *Herald-Examiner*

A Titan 2 rocket trails vapor as it hits the upper atmosphere after lunch at Cape Kennedy.

Auburn (N.Y.) *Citizen-Advertiser*

Several hundred blondes were dropped on Vietnam positions by thirty-six U. S. Air Force planes yesterday morning.

Fort Smith (Ark.) *Times Record*

Corporal Williams spent the first three days of his pass in bed with Flo.

Red Bluff (Calif.) *News*

On the afternoon of Saturday, February 25, over thirty women met at the home of Mrs. James W.

Lyons for the purpose of founding a De Pere Woman's club. The following permanent officers were elected: President, Mrs. James W. Lyons.

De Pere (Wisc.) *News*

Wanted: Reliable woman to take care of baby. Mrs. J. W. Lyons.

De Pere (Wisc.) *News*

New railroad law states that when two trains approach each other on the same track, both shall come to a full stop and neither shall proceed until the other has passed.

Chicago (Ill.) *Tribune*

Continued heavy rainfall would bring even more water.

Indianapolis (Ind.) *News*

"My husband's wife is a dear," said Norton's white-haired mother.

Los Angeles (Calif.) *Herald-Examiner*

A contest judge asked one of Mississippi's Miss Hospitality candidates recently: "What would you say if an outsider asked you why he should visit Mississippi?" "Because this is a hospitable state with a hostile people," the girl replied.

Hattiesburg (Miss.) *American*

Send four trucks to Fort Mason gym, 7:30 tonight, for hauling girls to dance. Bodies must be cleaned and seats wiped off.

Thomasville (Ga.) *Times-Enterprise*

He had to admire the way she did not change color. Though her head had dropped back on her throat.

Philadelphia (Pa.) *Saturday Evening Post*

So that was really the father of this baby! No use denying. Whom else would a man leave money secretly through his brother in a sealed envelope?

New York (N.Y.) *Times*

Gene Sloop, son of Mrs. Carl Sloop Jr. of Myrtle Street, celebrated his 100th birthday with a dinner party Monday evening. Present were his paternal grandparents, Mr. and Mrs. Carl Sloop Sr., his parents Mr. and Mrs. Carl Sloop Jr., and his sister, Miss Rebecca Sloop.

Salisbury (N.C.) *Post*

Municipal officials have decided to alter the spelling of this Hertfordshire town from Little Berkhampsted to Little Berkhampsted. "It sounds the same," said one, "but the new spelling is shorter."

London (Canada) *Free Press*

Among his patrons were the Emperor of Japan, the Emperor and Empress Dowager of China, the King of Siam, the Shah of Persia, the Sultan of Turkey and most of the crowded heads in Europe.

Philadelphia (Pa.) *Bulletin*

Tonight's shows:
9:00 Geo. Gobel Show
9:15 Geo. Gobel Shot

Nashville (Tenn.) *Banner*

Have your wedding announced, or have your question concerning weddings answered, by Mary Miller on her television program, "Wedding Bells," Sundays, Channel 13, 11:40 a.m. Also to be broadcast will be news concerning Mary Miller's Packaged Wedding Plan that provides brides with the best wedding possible for only $150,000 for the wedding, plus 30¢ per guest at the reception.

Houston (Tex.) *Chronicle*

We had Harold Smithers listed as absent last week. He was present and we are sorry.

St. Louis (Mo.) *Pepper Box*

A crowd estimated at 700 turned out last night to witness the burning of approximately 2,000 discarded members of the Athol Chamber of Commerce.

Worcester (Mass.) *Telegram*

Upon expiration of his leave he will report to Mare Island for 18 months' snore duty.

Aurora (Mo.) *Advertiser*

Have you noticed fresh scratches on your furniture? If so, try this simple remedy. Dip a walnut meat in salt and rub on the marks. The oil of the walnut will color the scratches and they will fade from sight.

Throw it away!

Las Vegas (Nev.) *Sun*

The freeway will be open to public travel tomorrow and is expected to afford considerable east-west traffic congestion.

San Mateo (Calif.) *Times*

Mrs. Irene Manning went to Bellingham last week to complete the purchase of material for her new home. She returned with a Chevrolet sedan.

Friday Harbor (Wash.) *Journal*

Send your name and address on a postcard. We will tell you where you can purchase our fine garden mixture. All you have to do is use a small amount of water, mix and pray regularly.

Little Rock (Ark.) *Democrat*

To assure absolute impartiality the judges will be awarded as prizes.

New York (N.Y.) *Telegraph*

I like this boy a lot and he likes ma but he wants to be serious all the time.

San Diego (Calif.) *Independent*

The girls are inexperienced but are shaping up nicely.

Fredericksburg (Tex.) *Standard*

Desirability of marital law to give the United States Army full sway in relieving Louisville's flood victims was discussed today.

Birmingham (Ala.) *Post Herald*

Do not exceed 5 miles per hour over bridge BB204 located ¾ mile west of Elso on account of the bridge having been removed.

Laramie (Wyo.) *Boomerang*

Mrs. Britton I. Budd, one of the many who took turns presiding at the tea table.

Chicago (Ill.) *Sunday Tribune*

The New York Yankees have signed their three-man coaching staff of Frank Crosetti, Bill Dickey and Jim Turner, the club announced Sunday. This marks the seventh straight season the Yanks have signed their coaching staff intact. Shot one Monday.

Olean (N.Y.) *Times Herald*

When he reached San Francisco, it suddenly occurred to him that he had neglected to visit one of the ports of call named in the sailing orders he had issued to himself. So what did Cap'n Ed do but turn back on his tracks and steer southeastward for the Hawaiian Islands!

San Francisco (Calif.) *Chronicle*

About 200 people were present for the dinner party, some of them were ladies.

Oklahoma City (Okla.) *Oklahoman*

Hawaiian Salad

One pint thinly sliced crisp cabbage, one cup pineapple cut in cubes, one tart red apple, one-fourth cup preserved finger cut in small pieces.

El Paso (Tex.) *Times*

On Wednesday evening Mrs. Nina Ford was hostess at a lonely dinner party, given in honor of her sister Mrs. Nora Staples.

Milford (Pa.) *Dispatch*

Rescuers fought to have scores of injured persons trapped in the debris, and dug out bodies.

New York (N.Y.) *Post*

Using a soup spoon and a table knife, a prisoner broke out of the ancient Colusa County jail last night. The old jail has had several escapes. Julie Gariby went through a skylight in 1054 and is still missing.

San Francisco (Calif.) *Examiner*

The star witness against both Mooney and Billings has a unique record for lying, if anyone can believe him.

Berkeley (Calif.) *Gazette*

Edward Worden, 35, was killed yesterday in a collision between his cat and that of Al Longley.

Bay City (Mich.) *Daily Times*

A terrific task awaits the Iowa University Hawkeyes here tonight as they aim to snap a three-game losing streak against the nation's highest demo sports 2-24 displays set italice head bold face cut scoring basketball team, Ohio State.

Davenport (Iowa) *Democrat*

Torrential rains have flooded several districts in southern Spain. In Malaga much damage was done to the almond, grape and the Archbishop of Canterbury.

Columbus (Ohio) *Dispatch*

It took many rabbits many years to write the Talmud.

Holland (Mich.) *Evening Sentinel*

Sam Hoskins accidentally shot himself while hunting. One of the wounds is fatal but his friends are glad to hear that the other one is not serious.

Winnebago City (Minn.) *Enterprise*

All the shops are shut, the streets are decked with flags and at night the village squire is illuminated.

Boston (Mass.) *Traveler*

Open house will be held at the museum next Sunday to introduce Sam Hutto and the opening of a two-weeks art show featuring his most decent works.

Macon (Ga.) *Telegraph and News*

She has studied piano, organ, voice, saxophone and rums.

Grand Forks (N.D.) *Herald*

Dr. and Mrs. George F. Taylor recently were guests in San Fernando of Dr. and Mrs. William Byers, and at Cal Tech they visited Dr. and Mrs. L. Muehlner. Another free week end was spent at Yosemite skiing.

Los Gatos (Calif.) *Times-Saratoga Observer*

"There just isn't enough silver to go around," Pastore said. "It makes no sense to continue with silver in the half dollar when we're getting rid of it in the dime and 10 and 25 cent pieces."

Fort Smith (Ark.) *Southwest American*

According to the new procedure in the County Finance Department, the bank president has been authorized to make monthly advances to Miss Morrison.

Memphis (Tenn.) *Commerical Appeal*

Watson, inventor of the new instrument, said the idea came to him while lying on a park wench in Chicago.

Chicago (Ill.) *Tribune*

During the lunch, Honorable Gelle took the toast of the newly married couple.

Denver (Colo.) *Rocky Mountain News*

The store room in the Whittier National Trust & Savings Bank building is being remodeled and equipment is being installed for a she store.

Whittier (Calif.) *News*

Plans were also revealed for the immediate start of construction of a 110,000 square foot plant in Miami to produce a $10 million a year volume of pleasure in 23 foot to 60 foot lengths.

Miami (Fla.) *Herald*

A baby at Great Warley, England, has living four grand-parents, four great-grand-parents, and two great-great-grand children.

Denver (Colo.) *Post*

Mrs. Franklin Pearce is resting nicely in the hospital after having a guitar removed from her neck by a specialist in San Antonio.

Eagle Pass (Tex.) *Guide*

Miss Deborah Wilkins and Mr. Ronald Hawkins visited the courthouse yesterday. While they were there, they received a bedding license from the County Clerk.

Chattanooga (Tenn.) *News*

Background files show that Clements was the co-founder of the Townsend Plan with F. E. Townsend in 1933. The plan, which has faded into history after having masses of followers at one time, called for federal prisons for all elderly persons.

Houston (Tex.) *Post*

A fourth-grade pupil is recovering from the effects of being accidentally choked to death.

Newark (N.J.) *Star-Ledger*

Jeff Hinze made a business trip to Central City Friday. He returned with a new top on his car which was destroyed by fire some time ago.

Albion (Nebr.) *Boone Companion*

Some people claim the most beautiful legs in the world belong to Mme. Alexandra Danilova of the Ballet Russe de Monte Carlo. With the idea of settling this argument, I picked up my camera and went up to Mme. Danilova's Toronto hotel room. I was determined to come away with a photograph of her legs, or bust.

Montreal (Canada) *Standard*

The club stables contain six horses and members can go deep-sea fishing if they feel the urge.

Honolulu (Hawaii) *Star-Bulletin*

Others hold the view that school parties after school parties are either unnecessary, undesirable or both.

Albany (N.Y.) *Times-Union*

Honorable mentions in the school science fair were Tim Culbertson with the anatomy of a chicken, and Robert Frank with the nervous system of an earthworm.

Marianna (Fla.) *Jackson County Floridan*

Sorry to report that Hubert (Slim) Campbell is recuperating at his home.

Terre Haute (Ind.) *Tribune*

Drunk pedestrians get killed oftener than drunk drivers.

Claremont (Calif.) *Sentinel*

The minister was covered with papers and other rubbish, then drenched with gasoline and set afire. The murderer then set the entire house afire . . . more sports on page 7.

Louisville (Ky.) *Times*

Undress rather than overdress for any occasion. You're less conspicuous.

Troy (N.Y.) *Times Record*

The Central Airc___ Company is producing the smallest motor-car ev.r made, but with very powerful engines. It is said that these cars can climb the steepest pedestrians.

New York (N.Y.) *Telegraph*

Miss Roberta Ford was injured while driving a car near this city yesterday. The area in which Miss Ford was injured is spectacularly scenic.

Monterey (Calif.) *Peninsula Herald*

She and her husband protected their three children by throwing themselves on the youngsters.

Little Rock (Ark.) *Gazette*

For everyone filing a tax return—sensational new kit contains 12 separate envelopes for organized filing of all income and expense tax vouchers, and padded cash voucher slips.

St. Louis (Mo.) *Globe-Democrat*

The Tuesday matinee at the Arcadia Theater will be on Saturday this week instead of Thursday.

Wellsboro (Pa.) *Gazette*

Jerome Cartwright was severely bitten on the hand by a cold Saturday which he was breaking.

Vale (Ore.) *Enterprise*

Two bullets ended the latest wolf, coyote or wild dog scare in Detroit. The next will appear in an early issue.

Detroit (Mich.) *News*

Mr. Melvin C. Holland and Mr. Donald Eakin, Science and Vocational Agriculture teachers, respectfully, each have two year sexperience at Douglass.

Nacogdoches (Tex.) *Daily Sentinel*

Mrs. Whitman is suffering from complications at her home.

Sioux Falls (S.D.) *Argus-Leader*

After finding out that he had a wife in West Virginia, she shot her liver with a pistol.

St. Louis (Mo.) *Post-Dispatch*

This is the time of year for the Palmyra Community Chest Drive. Remember you are supporting not one worthwhile agency. Give accordingly!

Palmyra (N.Y.) *Timesaver*

Mrs. Williams is another Iowan who increases California's population during the winter months.

Eagle Grove (Iowa) *Eagle*

The guests will enter the main door into the lobby of the Consistory, where after checking their garments, they will pass in double line to the beautiful drawing-room.

Buffalo (N.Y.) *News*

Colorful square handkerchiefs of chiffon or fine silk are now being sold for evening wear as much as sports wear.

Honolulu (Hawaii) *Star-Bulletin*

Mr. Delbert Fenton and Miss Florence Miles were at the marriage license bureau yesterday. Mr. Fenton is forty-five years of age and Miss Miles says she is twenty-five.

Lancaster (Ohio) *News-Review*

Mrs. Ida Gochenour was bitten last week by a dog which required some medical treatment.

Luray (Va.) *News and Courier*

James Ignatius Faherty, 44, one of the Boston Brink's robbery suspects, still at large, has been added to the FBI's list of "10 most wanted men." He has a better than average vocabulary and is considered extremely dangerous.

Detroit (Mich.) *News*

After working all day Sunday in his office, he was stricken during the evening, and it was announced today that his disposition had been diagnosed as an inflamed appendix.

Orlando (Fla.) *Sentinel*

Mrs. Y. C. Autrey is suffering as primary teacher in the Lamison school.

Selma (Ala.) *Times-Journal*

One of their two dogs was acquired in Connecticut and the other joined the family in Everitt. "We wet around," he admits.

Wenatchee (Wash.) *World*

Two and a half hours later she was on the stage being presented a gold-plated lifetime pass for two, and getting a kiss from Liberace to boot.

Liberace to boot.

Kansas City (Mo.) *Times*

Mayor John F. Dore of Seattle believes in taking plenty of his own financial medicine when it comes to cutting salaries and wages. Last year he reduced his salary from $1,500 to $5,000 a year.

Oakland (Calif.) *Tribune*

Houses and structures that were condemned and either ordered demolished, together with their owners or agents, are herewith listed.

Memphis (Tenn.) *Press-Scimitar*

A new free bridge to connect Missouri and Kansas will be opened July 1st at St. Joseph, Mich.

Lafayette (Ind.) *Journal and Courier*

Where there were 22 bookkeeping departments before, there are only five today and at the touch of a few buttons the machines tell each branch exactly how much cash and securities it must have. All that remains is to take physical inventory.

New York (N.Y.) *Herald Tribune*

Mr. and Mrs. William Redman and family were week-end guests in the R. W. Rabbitt hole in Sioux City.

Alton (Iowa) *Democrat*

He had the privilege also of viewing a number of rare Egyptian tummies.

Cleveland (Ohio) *Suburban News*

He suffered a fracture of the right nose in the crash.

Elizabeth (N.J.) *Daily Journal*

Many in the audience were aware of the fact they were seeing the same sow that 2,900 New Yorkers were turned away from when it played Carnegie Hall.

Melville (Canada) *Advance*

He seized her by the air and pulled her head back over the seat.

Dallas (Tex.) *Times-Herald*

Bles followed the patrolman to the sidewalk, where they say Johnson whipped out his pencil, beat Bles over the head with it, knocked him unconscious to the sidewalk and continued beating him so brutally that bystanders protested.

New York (N.Y.) *Sun*

The head teller celebrated his 50th year with the bank and was still going wrong.

Shreveport (La.) *Journal*

Strang took his followers to Beaver Island in Lake Michigan, called himself King Strang, and set up an independent kingdom. He had five wives, but otherwise was reputed to be a wise and learned man.

Cleveland (Ohio) *Plain Dealer*

When discovering the blaze, George Nichols, aged 5, rushed to the front of the house where his grandfather was sleeping. Awakening the old gentleman, he picked up a trunk and knocked the ¬indow-screen and sash out, helping his grandfather to safety through the upstairs window.

Altoona (Pa.) *Mirror*

Mr. and Mrs. Fred Goss will host a small cocktail party in their garden Tuesday before taking guests to dinner at Cafe Del Rey Moro. The group will go late to the symphony concert.

San Diego (Calif.) *Union*

Do not stick skewers, knives or folks in your roa[] too soon, as all natural juices will drain out and spo[] its flavor.

Sarasota (Fla.) *News*

After he joined up with George Washington in th[] Revolution, Lafayette was practically a commuter be[] tween France and the United States. Following h[] original visit, he came back here again in 1780, 178[] 1824 and 1925.

New York (N.Y.) *Journal-American*

To relieve congestion, take Astoria ferry every fif[] teen minutes.

Jamaica (N.Y.) *Long Island Press*

Games, this season, will be played as usual at Sea[] view Park, which is on the ocean front every Thurs[] day and Saturday.

Cape May (N.J.) *Star and Wave*

The purpose of the luncheon was to thank Mrs[] Wickham for her cooperation and for starting the year[] off right. She has resigned as president.

Carmichael (Calif.) *Westerner*

The recent case of attempted tire robbery, at White's[] lunch room near Sewickly bridge, was quietly dis[] posed of, it being shown that the accused, Lawrence[] Kaufmann, of New Kensington, came from very good[] people and was drunk when he came.

Pittsburgh (Pa.) *Press*

126

Charles F. Reynolds, former Pawtucket mayor, sat on his first case today as state liquor control administrator.

Providence (R.I.) *Bulletin*

For the second time in six months a high school student was killed in an auto accident.

Killdeer (N.D.) *Herald*

The winner in Boston will meet the Los Angeles Lakers, who won the Western Division title Tuesday night in Baltimore by holding off a late rally by the Bullets for a 117–115 victory. As if cheering on his squad, Schayes said: LOUIS WEINBERGER CAN TAILOR A SUIT TO FIT YOU PERFECTLY.

Fort Smith (Ark.) *Southwest American*

Stir in about two-thirds of the buttered and floured muffin pans and bake 25 minutes in a hot oven (400 degrees F.).

Washington (D.C.) *Star*

Rainfall yesterday and last night totaled .56 of an inch downtown and .47 of an inch at the Seattle-Tacoma Airport. The rain was needed for dry farmlands and forecasts.

Seattle (Wash.) *Times*

The Young People's organization is most encouraging. Last Sunday night there were 19 present, and one appeared to enjoy the meeting thoroughly.

Marion (N.C.) *Church Bulletin*

The W.C.T.U. will meet at 7:30 Thursday night at the church to discuss plans for the coming year. slug slug slug slug

Syracuse (N.Y.) Journal

The danger arising from an open season on deer lies in the fact that when a deer falls to earth, killed or injured, there is a good chance of the egg lying on the ground, dormant, until the following spring, and then hatching.

Tallahassee (Fla.) Democrat

A cold spell struck Jimtown last week and Bootlegger Ike Stubbs had to put alcohol in his liquor to keep it from freezing.

Chicago (Ill.) Associated Editors

The groom-to-be's mother has invited many friends to her Hollywood home for 5 to 7 cocktails.

Los Angeles (Calif.) Times

Among some of the people Miss Blank has painted was the Viscountess Curzon, called the most beautiful woman in London. She has pained a number of well-known Americans as well, and once was commanded to the royal palace.

New York (N.Y.) Evening World

He told of the viewpoint of the engineer, how he sits in the cab of his engine with one hand on the throttle and the other glued on the track ahead.

St. Petersburg (Fla.) Times

One of the judges disclosed it was her reserved baring, plus her intelligence, that helped swing the title to her.

Huntington (W. Va.) *Advertiser*

The young people of the First Baptist Church will have a little pet-together at the church parlors on Friday evening. A light lunch will be served afterwards.

Lincoln (Nebr.) *Journal-Star*

For many days and weeks thereafter Maria awaited his return. Each new football that echoed on the polished tiles would send her heart to beating rapidly.

Knoxville (Tenn.) *Journal*

But we try to avoid the fraction that might come from being together too much.

Newton (Kan.) *Kansan*

I was brought up on a farm. Trees would produce fruit according to their nature—some early, some later. Grain was left on the tree until a golden color.

Boston (Mass.) *Traveler*

Truck production is 15 percent ahead of a year ago; car putput is up about 6 percent.

New York (N.Y.) *Times*

Kenneth J. Smith, leader of the Philadelphia Ethical Society, will address the Platform Meeting of the Westchester Ethical Society at 11 a.m. on the topic "The

Playboy Magazine—Philosophy of Life and Sex Evaluated." There will be no Sunday School tomorrow.

Mount Vernon (N.Y.) *Argus*

F. Clark Parnell, son of Mr. and Mrs? Z. O. Parnell, has left for the Mexico Military Institute.

Tulsa (Okla.) *Tribune*

Class Q allotments are based upon the number of dependents up to a maximum of three, so, if the birth of a child will mean your husband is entitled to more quarters allowance, notify him to take the necesssary action.

St. Louis (Mo.) *Globe-Democrat*

Television Schedule:
9:00 P. M.

4—People's Choice
5—Wrestling
7—Star Tonight
9—Five Against Crime
11—Police Call
13—Boring

New York (N.Y.) *Post*

Most of these people, we believe, don't like the idea of a Soviet-daminated Europe.

Claremont (N.H.) *Daily Eagle*

Other celebrats were Candy Parsons, 6, and Sandra Martyn, 5.

Santa Monica (Calif.) *Evening Outlook*

The Missionary Circle will meet at Mrs. DuMez Friday afternoon. After meeting they will have a birthday party in honor of Mrs. L. McCauley. This will be a surprise to her.

Moorhead (Minn.) *Forum-News*

Eagle River's centennial is the biggest celebration ever planned by the community and may not again be repeated for some time.

Eagle River (Wisc.) *Vilas County News-Review*

Myrtle French is staging a vigorous fight for a public rest room for this city of 35,000 persons. The Women's Relief Corps has been backing Myrtle.

Des Moines (Iowa) *Register*

Souville sighed comfortably, seated himself on his chest, and folded his plump hands across his melon-like stomach.

Philadelphia (Pa.) *Inquirer*

Rev. A. J. and Mrs. Prosser say they had a dandy time out at their place last Thursday when 35 Baptist clergymen each with 35 wives broke in on them for a picnic.

Phoenix (Ariz.) *Church Bulletin*

The politician stated that as he looked over the vast audience he saw many faces he would like to shake hands with.

Muskogee (Okla.) *Phoenix*

They will comb the country for an "unknown" to portray the role of the "panther woman" in the "Island of Lost Souls." The girl selected must be 17, and not more than 30 years old.

Houston (Tex.) *Chronicle*

Information as to the owners of the dogs would be appreciated, as they should be either killed or restrained from doing further damage.

Atascadero (Calif.) *News*

Rep. Short (R-Mo.) has accepted invitations to deliver two high school commencement addresses in his home state.

They are at Exeter, May 12 and the hallway outside.

Springfield (Mo.) *Leader & Press*

Eugene Jones, who has been in poor health, is gaining rapidly under the treatment he is now taking. He is at work.

Cincinnati (Ohio) *Times-Star*

Will the ladies of the Willing Workers of Presbyterian Church who have towels which belong to the kitchen please bring them to the Church on Friday as we need them for supper.

East Rochester (N.Y.) *Herald*

State Senator Ernest A. Johnson, seeking re-election said, "I have made no wild promises, except one —honest government."

Worcester (Mass.) *Sunday Telegram*

A screaming crowd of 200 men and women tonight attempted to lynch Holland. Two police defended the prisoner until refreshments arrived.

Honolulu (Hawaii) *Star-Bulletin*

Mr. DeWitt visited the school yesterday and lectured on "Destructive Pests!" A large number were present.

Grand Rapids (Mich.) *Press*

Woellner is director of the university's guidance and placement center, established to help students to avoid becoming round pigs in square holes in later life.

Columbus (Ohio) *Dispatch*

To keep cats from straying, stay with them outdoors for the first month or so.

Washington (D.C.) *Post & Times Herald*

The payment of $90 is urged in full settlement of Eugene Yutterman, who fell on an allegedly icy health officer and clerk.

Hartford (Conn.) *Courant*

Fred Ferd, Canadian fur-trapper, fought and killed seven grizzly bears barehanded. Unfortunately, he was fighting eight at the time.

Chicago (Ill.) *Tribune*

The bride was given in marriage by her brother, Col. W. Day. Miss Daisy Day was the dog, and the latter is being kept under observation by the health authorities.

Toronto (Canada) *Globe*

The marriage of Miss Anna Held and Willis Turner, which was announced in this paper a few weeks ago, was a mistake and we wish to correct.

Alamosa (Colo.) *News*

Her Majesty has seen so many fine clothes worn in Europe that she would be delighted to see Americans in their native dress.

New York (N.Y.) *World*

Lovely legs can be a great asset to a woman and one that lasts much longer than just a pretty face. With the fashion cycle swinging back to the short skirts of the 20's, it will be good to see slim graceful legs replacing the ample bosoms that have been so popular recently.

Los Angeles (Calif.) *Times*

At this writing Miss Mary Briscoe is much better. The family has our deepest sympathy.

Ashdown (Ark.) *Little River News*

"Street of Memories," Guy Kibbee, Lynn Roberts. Amnesia victim on Skid Row is befriended by a girl, but when he regains his memory, he forgets her.

Los Angeles (Calif.) *Times*

Mrs. George Earl, who gave birth to a 19-year-old daughter is reported as getting along fine. A. J. Dill, of Farley, who also suffered a broken leg in the same accident, is recovering.

Moran (Tenn.) *Times*

There has been more good legislation in behalf of the asses in the last 20 years than in the last 5000 years.

Lumpkin (Ga.) *News*

"Green Stockings," a three-act play, will be presented in the Immanuel Episcopal Church. Robert Morrey has been directing the cats.

New Haven (Conn.) *Register*

For slippers, we vote for braided sandals of gold kid, very nudist, and you can forego hose and manicure your tonsils if you want to.

Birmingham (Ala.) *Post Herald*

She made an unscheduled and sudden departure from the saddle, head first, into the drink. Her mouth stayed behind.

Atlanta (Ga.) *Journal*

The matron of honor was Mrs. C. M. Spivey, and the beset man was Walker Grenade.

Atlanta (Ga.) *Constitution*

The missing woman is described a strikingly pretty blonde with long black hair.

New York (N.Y.) *Times*

Rubenstein was found dying on the pavement with his skull crushed and his throat cut by a passer-by a few moments after the accident.

Washington (D.C.) *Star*

Her only souvenirs today are earrings and a pendant necklace fashioned of gold nuggets and a sourdough husband.

Seattle (Wash.) *Post-Intelligencer*

Cats weigh 34 pounds to the bushel compared to 60 pounds for a bushel of wheat.

Medford (Mass.) *Daily Mercury*

In spite of the fact that the judge said he would be lenient with a man who had committed bigamy, the poor fellow was allowed to go free.

Nashville (Tenn.) *Tennessean*

Poetry, under the capable leadership of Mrs. J. H. Collins, was cussed from various angles.

Lakeland (Fla.) *Ledger*

A soft-ball game of the All-Star girls team against the All-Star boys team was stopped when one of the girls complained the male pitcher was pinching low.

Fresno (Calif.) *Bee*

Judge Bentley, one of our most eligible bachelors, is retiring from politics. Hale, hearty and 55, the Judge says he wants a little peach and quiet.

Corliss (Calif.) *Journal*

Enlarging the width and depth of the canal is expected to relieve some of the constipation so often experienced by tug-line owners in the past.

Albany (N.Y.) *Times-Union*

Gov. Robert E. Meyner will start the $75,000 campaign with a dinner speech Tuesday evening. It will run one month.

New York (N.Y.) *Times*

The two movie stars were married June 4th in the Hollywood Methodist Church while a hundred policemen held back the large crow.

New York (N.Y.) *Times*

Least, but not last on the program was Mrs. George Sharpe.

Steubenville (Ohio) *Herald-Star*

Mrs. Williamson was betwitching in black lace.

Raleigh (N.C.) *Times*

A 16-month-old girl died when the family car curled up on top of her head and dozed off.

Austin (Tex.) *American*

He has always received condemnation from both sides for his fair and impartial handling of all cases.

San Diego (Calif.) *Union*

Night watchman W. H. Butts, making his rounds, tried the front door and found it unlocked. Then he gave a peculiar growl and bark, and every hair on his body grew stiff.

Kerman (Calif.) *News*

After a conference today, the Police Chief announced that "if Sally appears nude she will be arrested and so will the management. There will be an officer at every performance to see that there are no slips."

Chicago (Ill.) Tribune

Geraldine Farrar, opera star, who has announced that she will retire from the concert stage when she is fifty years old, says that she believes the older generation of sinners should give way gracefully to the younger.

Monroe (La.) Morning Post

Both Dr. and Mrs. Elwood Worcester were feeling better today after having been knocked down by an automobile.

Boston (Mass.) Transcript

I have lived here for a long time. Besides this, my wife has man interests here.

Birmingham (Ala.) News

Service at the Marcus post office got back to abnormal Monday with the return of Pat Collins from his annual vacation as chief clerk.

Marcus (Iowa) News

The New Jersey Senator and his wife were host to members of the family and several odd friends.

New York (N.Y.) Herald Tribune

The company will design and engineer the reactor for a $10.8 million unclear power project.

Washington (D.C.) Post

Anderson recently completed an instruction course in use of the array of electric woodworking tools manufactured by the Porter-Cable Machine Co., at Syracuse, N. Y. He will have charge of all instruction and promotion for the fools in this area.

Meadville (Pa.) *Tribune*

One length of nose can be made to do the work of three or more by inserting special spraying nozzles at intervals. These distribute a fine mist in all directions.

Toronto (Canada) *Daily Star*

A theater party marked the 11th birthday celebration of Robert Clark Curtis when several of his friends attended the Sunday matinee before heaving refreshments at his home.

Niles (Mich.) *Star*

He said "factories in the Soviet Union are producing twenty times more air-planes, motors and accessories than France." He said the factories were equipped principally with English and German machinery and employed about 200,000 working in three shirts.

St. Louis (Mo.) *Post-Dispatch*

In her first four motion pictures, she was the daughter of: Joan Crawford in "Possessed," Joan Bennett in "The Reckless Moment," and Fredric March in "An Act of Murder," and Errol Flynn's piece in "Cry Wolf."

Little Rock (Ark.) *Democrat*

A mass feeding exercise in which county Civil Defense volunteers cook meals under simulated disaster conditions has been postponed because of muddy ground near the CD headquarters here.

San Diego (Calif.) *Union*

Until recently the three services had a free hand to develop their own missies for their own missions.

Hartford (Conn.) *Times*

Imperial Potentate Earl C. Mills said etaoin shrdlu shrdlu etaoi shrdlu eatoin utaordlu uau ntaordlunt last night in a visit to the Kerbele Shrine Temple here.

Knoxville (Tenn.) *Journal*

The line of veterans, marching south on Main Street, in North Little Rock, presented an unusual spectacle, and dozens of automobiles drove slowly up and down the street gazing curiously at the men.

Little Rock (Ark.) *Gazette*

The Town and Country Garden Club will meet on Wednesday evening at 8 o'clock. Mrs. Ralph Dona and Mrs. Raymond T. Schmelzle will demonstrate the identification of bare limbs.

Le Roy (N.Y.) *Gazette-News*

"I love you, too," she cried, and swaying toward him threw herself into his arms. His lips found and clung to her sweet, tremendous mouth.

Minneapolis (Minn.) *Sunday Journal*

A beauty contest such as was held last year will be a feature of the celebration this year, the only difference being that the contestants will dispense with bathing suits.

Logan (Ohio) Republican

The Interstate Commerce Commission authorized Capital Transit Company, which mauls people around Washington, D. C., in street cars and buses, to split its capital stock.

Chicago (Ill.) Tribune

It is estimated that a block of wood containing twelve cubic inches will produce enough pulp for a twelve-page daily newspaper. It takes a slightly larger block, however, to produce the editorials.

New York (N.Y.) Post

In moving the adoption of his resolution, Assemblyman Streit charged that Prohibition has been a "terrible failure," that more persons are arrested today charged with intoxication than before the dry law was enacted, and that beer drinkers are filling the pails of the State.

New York (N.Y.) Times

Houchin also killed a doe on his hunting trip. He was accompanied by Paul Smith, who bagged a doe and a buck, and by Mrs. Bob Smith, mother of the latter.

Prescott (Ariz.) Courier

The Midland High Band will lead the parade next Saturday afternoon from the school to the athletic grounds. If it rains in the afternoon, the parade will be held in the morning.

Midland (Tex.) *Reporter-Telegram*

Not thrice but three times has lightning struck the barn on the Henry Summer farm.

Santa Cruz (Calif.) *News*

Blend sugar, flour and salt. Add egg and milk, cook until creamy in double boiler. Stir frequently. Add rest of ingredients. Mix well, serve chilled. Funeral services will be held Thursday afternoon at 2 o'clock.

Gettysburg (Pa.) *Times*

Mr. and Mrs. Vanderbeck and family, Mr. and Mrs. Robert Vanderbeck and family and Mr. and Mrs. Mayer all came out from Portland to eat Thanksgiving dinner at the home of their daughter, Mrs. A. Versteeg.

Newburg (Ore.) *Graphic*

The Ladies Night for the West Concord Bowling League will be held at the Concord Rod & Gun Club a week from Saturday night . . . so be sure and come, and bring the wife and girl friend.

Concord (Mass.) *Journal*

All persons are requested to clean up their premises and deposit same in the alleys. The city will furnish vehicles to haul some away.

Spearfish (S.D.) *News*

The Queen's first glimpse of the Capitol of the new world she entered upon today came as she stood, on the arm of Secretary of State Kellogg.

Schenectady (N.Y.) *Union-Star*

For my own part I have been cleaning orchards and truck patches and clearing out old blackberry patches and trying to get he hens to lay.

Coffeyville (Kan.) *Gazette*

After several bad decisions against the home team, many enraged fans in the bleachers started yelling "Kiss the Umpire!"

Nashville (Tenn.) *Tennessean*

When the freight came by, the water stopped pouring from the hose. The firemen looked back and discovered they had laid the house across the railroad tracks.

Norwalk (Conn.) *Hour*

We regret that we did not have the information about John Ehrlich correct. He is not an instructor, but fellow. Dr. Wolf is not head of the botany department. There is no botany department, it's in biology. It's not Durham University, but Duke University at Durham, North Carolina.

Ithaca (N.Y.) *Cornell Countryman*

W. M. Johnsons is walking about, but is complaining very much with his leg.

Heber Springs (Ark.) *Headlight*

Saturday they were married in the maternity ward of the hospital.

Boise (Idaho) *Evening Statesman*

This slim, frail-looking French woman is an accomplished sailor as well as the wife of Grands Magasins de Louvre, one of Paris's leading department stores.

Schenectady (N.Y.) *Gazette*

A great meeting is promised and all are asked to sacrifice pleasure and attend.

Louisville (Ky.) *Courier-Journal*

Mrs. Richard Hardesty will be hostess to members of Blocks to Books Mothers Club Wednesday evening at her home. "Which Shall I Be First, a Wife or a Mother?" is the question for a panel discussion.

Piqua (Ohio) *Call*

A drunkard of long standing has been reformed by an operation which removed a bone that pressed against the brain. The Detroit News also reports a number of cures effected by the removal of a brass rail that was pressing against the foot:

Kansas City (Mo.) *Star*

An ice jam from Niagara Falls threatened to floor Niagara Falls homes.

Chicago (Ill.) *Daily Tribune*

Mix and sift the dry ingredients and rub in the fat with the fingers or cut it in with a knife. Make a hole in the floor at the side of the bowl and add half a cupful of liquid.

New York (N.Y.) *Sun*

Hunters returning from the Colorado hunting trip reported killing a mouse weighing over 450 pounds.

Kansas City (Mo.) *Star*

Ashley Kendrick needed his handicap of 6 pints per game to defeat Cline Miyamoto for the championship of the Elks Club individual bowling tournament.

Saratoga (N.Y.) *Saratogian*

Special music was furnished by a trio composed of Mrs. H. M. Dace.

Harlingen (Tex.) *Valley Star*

Sermon:
9:15 & 10:45—"How Satin Slips Up on Us."

St. Petersburg (Fla.) *Times*

The FTC charged the Exquisite Form Brassiere Co., of New York City, with discriminating against its smaller customers.

Washington (D.C.) *News*

For perfect fit at the bustline, there are two points to consider.

Little Rock (Ark.) *Democrat*

The heavy cash burdens placed on large estates by the multiplicity of inheritance and estate taxes have made it dangerous for persons of wealth to die except in a bull market, and unless a large part of their estates is in liquid form.

New York (N.Y.) *Wall Street Journal*

He greeted her, during a court recess, with a hog and kisses.

Newark (Ohio) *Advocate*

One of the West 25th St. cafe owners phoned in. Kerr knew him, he had repeatedly cooperated with the police in their fight against law and order.

Toledo (Ohio) *Blade*

The explainers evidently come to the theater exclusively with morons as companions, so that the slightest twist of plot or entrance of a character has to be laboriously explained in a horse whisper.

Augusta (Ga.) *Chronicle*

A city ordinance banning the sale of phonographic literature was unanimously adopted at a meeting of the board of aldermen on March 12th. Persons convicted of dealing in phonographic literature can be given 30-day terms and/or fined $50.

Louisville (Ky.) *Courier-Journal*

Next Sunday: Mrs. Walters is the soloist at the morning service. The pastor will speak on "It's a Terrible Experience."

La Crescenta (Calif.) *Church Bulletin*

Joe Stenosklaip, of Streator, has just received a letter from his wife in Italy telling of the birth of a son.

Joe immediately set the boys up to drinks, and stated that he had not seen his wife for five years.

Washburn (Ill.) *Leader*

As Joan stepped into the police car Lowe flung a cat at her, which she donned for the ride to the City Jail.

Los Angeles (Calif.) *Herald-Examiner*

Alfred Hawkins of Harrisburg had the misfortune of getting hurt on his back and chest while milking this morning when a cow kicked. We wish her a speedy recovery.

Prairie Du Sac (Wisc.) *News*

A fire recently broke out in the Traverse City railway station waiting room. To the annoyance of the passengers their train came in just as the place was warming up.

Traverse City (Mich.) *Record-Eagle*

I would say that the average girl at 15 or 16 should be allowed to date as long as she is indiscreet.

Birmingham (Ala.) *I.*

He said Miss Hoffman originally came to Corpus Christi from Ilion, N. Y. She married a Navy man oooooooooooooooooooooe from whom she now is divorced.

Waco (Tex.) *News-Tribune*

Upon the trial of a cause in equity to cancel a deed from a husband to his deceased wife on the ground

147

that it was forged, the husband is incompetent to testify to matters occurring before his death.

Philadelphia (Pa.) *News*

All gardeners know, however fine are the plants they buy, it takes a bit of doing to bring them to full frustration.

Austin (Tex.) *American*

Miss Mina Morris was the fortunate winner of the twelve free greasings offered by the Callaway Service Station.

Birmingham (Ala.) *Post Herald*

Members of the Lions Club stretched and strained Thursday noon as Swan Johnson, local physical therapist, demonstrated deep-breathing exercises during the club meeting. There will be no meeting next week.

Tacoma (Wash.) *News-Tribune*

It was reported later that her husband was on his way to the Hall of Justice to boil her out.

San Francisco (Calif.) *Examiner*

At 7 and 9 p.m. in the Temple B'nai Israel, Rabbi Irving I. Hausman will speak on "In Spite of Everything."

Sacramento (Calif.) *Bee*

The Army and Air Force are being careful about the women they take into the WAC and WAF, but in spite of the restrictions many Kansas girls make the grade.

Abilene (Kan.) *Reflector-Chronicle*

"Ratings cannot measure intensity," he said. "Having your set on does not necessarily mean you are watching it. Watching a program does not necessarily mean you like it. Liking a program does not necessarily mean you care very much; it may mean you do not like it."

New York (N.Y.) *Times*

Mr. Khrushchev delivered the speech in Russian in a token manner, reading the first few lies only.

Calcutta (India) *Hindusthan Standard*

Anna Adcock celebrated her 100th birthday today with her husband John who will be 100 in 80 years.

Boston (Mass) *Herald*

Egyptian belly dancers cover up that part of her which other is that Conrad Hilton has made all men who want to work at his new Nile Hilton Hotel shave off their mustaches.

Brownsville (Tex.) *Herald*

"But the salary was good and I have a widowed mother living with men so I hesitated."

St. Joseph (Mo.) *News-Press*

Even so he would prefer a tent on the Gobi desert to a pesthouse on Manhattan.

Oklahoma City (Okla.) *Times*

"Why are merchants on the west side of Akard from Pacific to Jackson allowed to sweep refuse and rubbish into the butter at all times, night or day?"

Dallas (Tex.) *Times Herald*

All male persons between the ages of twenty-one and sixty, except those incapable of earning a support from being married or otherwise disabled.

Spartanburg (S.C.) *Herald*

He had a rigid schedule in late years, to bed at 6 p.m. and up at 7 p.m.

Lancaster (Pa.) *New Era*

Single leg balance. Standing balanced on the right leg, raise the other one to the side as high as you can, grasp the instep with the right hand and extend the other leg, raising the opposite hand with palm up in a graceful position.

New York (N.Y.) *Times*

Ambitious, fearless and tiresome, he fought his way up every rung on the ladder, making his own opportunities.

Ottawa (Canada) *Morning Journal*

This region has special problems because of its geography, its distance from the capital, and its swindling population.

New York (N.Y.) *Herald Tribune*

Today is Columbus Day, 469 years after Columbus landed on Plymouth Rock.

Olathe (Kan.) *News*

This telephoto was sent by the process of transmitting light wives from one sensitized cylinder to another.

Philadelphia (Pa.) *Bulletin*

The girls consisted of cigarettes, magazines, home-made candies, phonograph records, tobacco, chewing-gum, and candy bars.

Rhinelander (Wisc.) *News*

Burlingame bent over the paper. His eyes, filled with tears, dropped on the desk.

Washington (D.C.) *Post*

"They're poor, but free," he said. "We should keep them that way."

Hackensack (N.J.) *Record*

Bids received were from Burnham Brothers of Essex, $3,750, and from John A. Singer and Son of Ipswich, $4,500.
The selectmen voted to reject the kids. The local highway department will do the work.

Beverly (Mass.) *Times*

Everywhere that one looked could be seen strangers and non-strangers.

St. Louis (Mo.) *Post-Distpach*

Mr. and Mrs. Thomas Weekley highly entertained their daughter Wednesday night.

Muskogee (Okla.) *Times-Democrat*

The car was brought to a local garage for repairs and was badly damaged.

Galveston (Tex.) *Tribune*

Firemen were called to North Tenth Street between Main and Blondeau streets this morning, where an automobile had caught fire from a crossed wife in the car.

Keokuk (Iowa) *Gate City*

Family Night—A Gift for the Largest Family Present. Sermon: "Thou Fool."

York (Pa.) *Gazette and Daily*

The chorus was good, and the student orchestra played far better than could have been expected under the direction of Walter Ducloux.

Los Angeles (Calif.) *Times*

Mrs. Elsie McCutcheon of Westfield will speak on International Affairs at the Business and Professional Women's Club Thursday. Members who desire to cancel reservations should phone 288R.

Silver Creek (N.Y.) *Lake Shore News and Times*

Smith has written three Book-of-the-month selections. He says that he averages a book a month on his tripewriter.

Van Buren (Ark.) *Press Argus*

The special wedding reunion services for couple. married in Calvary Methodist Church will be held tomorrow morning. The Reverend R. C. Penrose will speak on "How Much Can You Endure?"

Pittsburgh (Pa.) *Post-Gazette*

A large crowd attended the meeting to hear the latest dope from Washington.

Little Rock (Ark.) *Democrat*

Rex Parsons laid an egg on our table that had been previously laid on the nest by a little white leghorn hen that was three inches in length and 6½ inches in circumference the smallest way.

Farmington (Me.) *Franklin Journal*

"It would sound like an alibi if I said I had a bar arm," the pitcher said.

New York (N.Y.) *Journal-American*

Spread of flames was prevented when a woman's glance out of a window brought fire-fighting equipment from the headquarters station.

Greenville (S.C.) *Piedmont*

It is the good fortune of Lyndon Johnson that he is a politician of enchanting capacity, capable not merely of seeing around corners but of simultaneously putting both ears to the ground.

New Haven (Conn.) *Register*

Tests at the University of Illinois have indicated that the sox of unknown writers can be revealed by examining their penmanship.

Dallas (Tex.) *Times Herald*

While it wasn't planned that way, it was nice that so many from the Baptist Church were in City Hospital at the same time last week.

Cambridge Springs (Pa.) *Enterprise-News*

A mysterious object about 10 feet in diameter hovered Monday above the bows of the vessel, Capt. Kaara Eakariassen reported Tuesday. The Captain, who was alone on board, remained for five minutes before rising rapidly out of sight.

Corpus Christi (Tex.) *Caller*

After a happy youth Mr. Kunkel settled down to a quite married life.

Baltimore (Md.) *Evening Sun*

R. Franze of the Wixon community was transacting business in Bryan Tuesday, incidentally shipping breeding poultry to other parts of the State. Mr. and Mrs. Franze enjoy the reputation of never having heard a word of complaint from a single bird they have shipped out.

Bryan (Tex.) *Eagle*

Seriously injured in an auto crash, Silas Steele is in a critical condition at Mercy Hospital. Dr. Reid happened on the scene soon after the accident, and applied quack first-aid treatment.

Salt Lake City (Utah) *Telegram*

The Skyland Garden Club will meet Thursday at 10 a.m. at the country club. Shady subjects will be discussed.

Tuscaloosa (Ala.) *News*

Judge Braxton sentenced a young man to nine months in the penitentiary for his confession of having stolen his mother's and several neighbor's chickens. Not being overly bright mentally, the Judge used clemency.

Aberdeen (S.D.) *American-News*

Married couples seeking a divorce in Illinois will have to go through a 60-day "cooing off" period.
Cleveland (Ohio) *Plain Dealer*

The new Deluxe Nite Coach will have sleeping accommodations for 25, and for daytime travel seating capacity for 40. Berths will be horizontal of the coach instead of vertical as on present models.
Mill Valley (Calif.) *Record*

Mrs. Stewart Vanderbilt beat off a bull that had attacked and knocked her husband unconscious with a pitchfork.
Peoria (Ill.) *Journal-Star*

Albert Johnson has returned to work after being laid off for five weeks because of an insured knee.
Newton (Kan.) *The Spotlight*

Judge Jones said witnesses had sworn to a warrant charging Dreiser and a young woman had liver together openly at a hotel.
Atlanta (Ga.) *Constitution*

Due to an error, Mr. and Mrs. Walter Thompson are the parents of a girl, born Wednesday morning in St. Mary's Mercy Hospital.
Chicago (Ill.) *Herald & Examiner*

If you are old enough to be married, you must see it. If you are not old enough to be married you cannot see it. Children under 12 free.
Philadelphia (Pa.) *News*

When Lucille Ball became president of Desilu Studios she had an office built into her

Owensboro (Ky.) *Messenger & Inquirer*

The estate was valued in the will at "more than $20,000." One-third goes to the widow and two-thirds to each of the children.

Washington (D.C.) *Evening Star*

A comely and well-dressed young woman, about 25 years old, was found unconscious shortly after midnight this morning in the Downtown theater. She was taken to the county hospital. Her condition was improved after her stomach had been jumped.

Chicago (Ill.) *Tribune*

Several men have entered the County Egg Laying Contest. If there are any others who desire to enter they are requested to notify Miss Ross at once.

Morrilton (Ark.) *Democrat*

A pretty home wedding was solemnized last evening at 5 o'clock when the daughter of Mr. and Mrs. John Williams became the bride of Mr. and Mrs. Herbert Richards, both of Bangor.

Easton (Pa.) *Express*

After nine days at sea, it's nice to feel a good, stanch desk under your feet again.

San Francisco (Calif.) *Chronicle*

Guest speaker will be Dr. Frank Sullivan of Loyola University. Dr. Sullivan will review his year at Oxford under a Ford.

Los Angeles (Calif.) *News Advertiser & Journal*

The givernment will provide $75 a month to the widow.

San Antonio (Tex.) *Light*

Mr. Adams said Dr. Sawyer would be welcomed at the nudist resort and would be permitted a first-visit prerogative of keeping his clothing on while he "looks around and sees the rear truth about nudism."

Battle Creek (Mich.) *Enquirer-News*

Miss Weinberger is a boy and arrow enthusiast and hopes to make a mark for herself in the sport.

Monroe (Va.) *World*

Stir 2 or 3 heaping teaspoons of instant cocoa mix in a glass of cola-flavored beverage for a cool treat. inside.

Hamilton (Bermuda) *Mid-Ocean News*

URGENT
1 LA
07

LOS ANGELES, AUG. 30 (AP) A SHARP EARTH SHOCK WAS FELT IN SEVERAL SECTIONS OF LOS ANGELES ABOUT 4 P.M. TODAY.

New York (N.Y.) *Times*

Miss Shirley Snyder is improving after an operation under which she went.

Carroll (Iowa) *Times Herald*

James McGillicuddy's Rolls-Royce was stolen while standing in front of the county poorhouse where he was visiting his aged parents.

Detroit (Mich.) *Free Press*

She slipped on a scatter rug and cut her face on a broken gallon of buttermilk.

Montgomery (Ala.) *Journal*

For entertainment during the rally, Miss Brown sang several songs and Mike McCormick played on his strumpet.

Fort Smith (Ark.) *News*

The nation's metropolis became a ghost town for 15 minutes Saturday in the biggest air raid drill since World War II. At 7:30 a.m. (CST) 579 sires wailed out in the clear morning.

Grand Island (Nebr.) *Independent*

Mrs. Mary Harper returned last Saturday night to find a skunk sitting in the middle of her kitchen. Mrs. Harper, being a resourceful person, got a squirt gun and opened a barrage of fly-spray. The skunk finally turned tail and bolted for the wide open spaces.

Mrs. Mary Harper left Sunday for a few weeks' visit with relatives and friends in Peoria.

Elwood (Ill.) *Gazette*

Police said between four and five bandits participated in the robbery.

Victoria (Canada) *Times*

The bride was attired in heavy white skinner satin, fashioned with a sweetheart neckline, fitted bodice, draped sleeves coming to points over the wrists, and a busted back.

Peekskill (N.Y.) *Evening Star*

Here is another on-the-pot dispatch by a science writer.

(New York, N.Y.) Associated Press

(Bath, England) Bath is short of water. After 16 days without rain, the city fathers announced an official drought and asked citizens to go east with the faucet.

Los Angeles (Calif.) *Examiner*

Miss Golden and her Astronomy class enjoyed an outdoor study period Tuesday night at which time three constellations were discussed at length, The Big Bear, Little Bear and the Big Diaper.

Mount Ramos (Ky.) *Citizen-Journal*

Milton Berle, the radio and screen comedian, and Joyce Mathews, New York showgirl, were on their wedding trip today. They were married at a quiet ceremony yesterday, attended only by a few loose friends and relatives.

San Francisco (Calif.) *Examiner*

The Men's Bible Class enjoyed a box social at the home of Ben Richardson, Wednesday night. The high spot of the evening's entertainment was a corset solo by Mrs. Richardson.

Benton (Ark.) *News*

Today's Sermon:
    "How Much Should A Christian Drink?"
    Hymns by a Full Choir.

Wilmington (Del.) *News*

Tomorrow . . . Annual Apple Festival in Community Center, 1 to 4 p.m. Homemade apple products. Worm apple pie at snack bar.

Ithaca (N.Y.) *Journal*

He told officers he started beating his wife while she was asleep with a leg of a dinette table.

San Antonio (Tex.) *Express*

Not a roll of toilet paper was on the shelves of eight of the city's largest grocery stores today. CR844A

Four thousand pounds of Epsom Salts will be offered for sale July 15, the War Assets Administration regional director said today. CR845A

(Houston, Tex.) United Press

Mrs. Carlisle, described as a "well-known and successful author," declared that prior to Dec. 7, 1941, she circulated her navel unsuccessfully among various motion picture producers.

Chicago (Ill.) *Tribune*

A colored woman stood before Magistrate Harry W. Allers in police court with a black eye.

Baltimore (Md.) *Evening Sun*

Mr. Davis testified he was not aware that his wife was running a charge account until last August when she came home from a millinery shop with a hot box.

San Diego (Calif.) *Tribune*